Discover Your Dorset Ancestors

A Guide to Dorset Records

What they are and where to find them

Chloe O'Shea

BSc (Hons), MA

Published by
The Family History Partnership
the publishing imprint of the
Family History Federation
P.O. Box 62
Sherringham, Norfolk
NR26 9AR

ISBN: 978 1 906280 61 1

First published 2022

Printed by Henry Ling Limited
The Dorset Press
Dorchester DT1 1HD

Dedication

This book is dedicated to my family;
past, present and future

Acknowledgments

I would like to thank the following people for their help, advice, encouragement and contributions towards this book.

Mum and Dad (Julie and Rodney Osmond)
James O'Shea
Ian Waller and the Family History Federation
Suzie Woodward, proofreader
Rita Pettet and the Somerset & Dorset Family History Society,
Sheila Martin and Dorset Family History Society
Luke Dady and Jacqui Halewood from Dorset History Centre

Credit is also due to:
Ancestry
FindMyPast
The Genealogist
British Newspaper Archive
Dorset Online Parish Clerks

Contents

Map of Dorset and Surrounding Counties

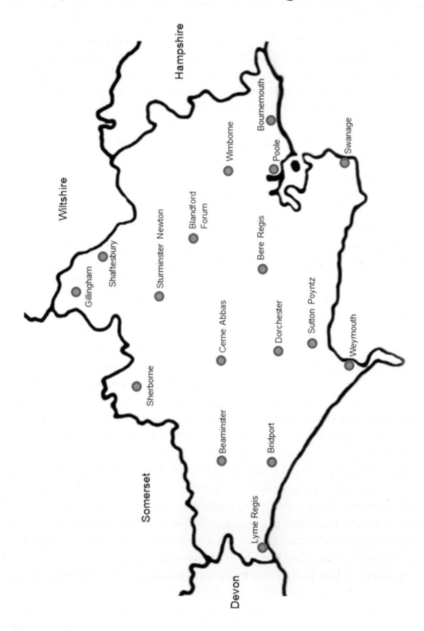

Introduction

Researching your family tree is hugely rewarding, providing people with a glimpse into their history and a sense of belonging. For those of us with Dorset ancestry, we are lucky enough to feel a bond with one of the most beautiful counties in England which has a rich history of farming, literature and seafaring. My own ancestry can be traced back to a wide variety of counties including Kent, Lancashire, Buckinghamshire and even a distant line back to Scotland; however, it is with my Dorset ancestors that I feel the greatest connection.

Having lived in Dorset for over twenty years, I have a great love for the county. When you have visited a place where your ancestors have lived, it helps to give you a sense of understanding of their lives, such as the views they would have seen that have remained unchanged and the distance they travelled on foot or by horse. However, when you have lived in the county it gives you an even bigger appreciation of what it means to truly be 'from Dorset'.

This book brings together the most useful records that can be used to trace your Dorset family tree. Many of the records are generic and can be found in most counties, but each record will feature an example of an ancestor from Dorset to show you how valuable the record can be for your research. There are also records which can only be found in Dorset which are often overlooked.

If you have not done so already, gather together all of your inherited family paraphernalia and study each document to make sure you have gained as much information as possible from the sources already in your possession. These may include postcards, photographs, certificates, licences, school records and letters amongst other memorabilia. Scan them in and save them digitally in at least two different places to avoid loss. Looking through these items gives you a good base from which to begin your research. If it has been a while since you last looked through these items, consider going back to them for another look. You may notice something that you missed the first time around.

Make sure you ask questions of family members who may be able to give you key pieces of information that you can use to trace your tree. I began tracing my family tree after the death of my grandfather, Robert Eggelton. It was when I was helping to clear his house in Lytchett Matravers that I came across a small handwritten family tree that initially aroused my interest. There are so many questions I would love to have asked him about his youth, his family and his time as a soldier. Sadly, when we lose those close to us, we also lose an awful lot of knowledge and memories that can no longer be passed on.

A majority of people reading this book will be familiar with records such as the census returns and documents of civil registration. There are chapters on these topics for those who are unfamiliar with them. The main focus of this book is to look at the lesser known records that can often be missed, such as title deeds, manorial records and maps. These records can often seem daunting if you have not come across them before, but this book will tell you where to find the records relating to Dorset and how to extract the most useful information from them.

This book is designed so that you can dip in and out of any chapter that you wish to read. Not every record will apply to each of your ancestors and some of the records may not feature your family at all. Title deeds can be particularly hard to source and many have not survived. However, where they do exist, they can be of huge significance to your research, perhaps even taking you back a further generation. Manorial records can be amongst some of the hardest to find and understand, but with a little time and practice, they can tell us a great deal about the daily lives of our ancestors. The value and limitations of each source will be clarified so you can understand their strengths and weaknesses with relation to genealogical research.

The Poole, Bournemouth and Christchurch area was transferred from Hampshire to Dorset in 1974 as a result of the Local Government Act 1972; this area is included in the book for the benefit of people researching their ancestry from here. Many records for this area are retained by Hampshire Record Office so bear this in mind when you are researching those ancestors as it may be necessary to search *their* catalogue rather than that of Dorset History Centre. When researching your more recent ancestors, remember that due to confidentiality laws in England, you will be unable to access certain documents from the last 100 years.

Most of the examples used in this book feature my own ancestors who largely hail from Sutton Poyntz, Osmington, Swanage and Poole but I have endeavoured to feature other examples from across the county to provide a broader interest to those of you with ancestors from other parts of the county.

I hope this book encourages you to find out more about your family tree using records that not only provide names and dates, but that also give us a sense of who are ancestors were, their characters and what their lives were like all those years ago in the glorious county of Dorset.

1. The author in Osmington churchyard.

CHAPTER 1
Civil Registration

About the Record

Civil Registration documents are certificates of birth, marriage and death, often referred to as BMD certificates. They form the first part of our research, helping us to trace back from ourselves, generation by generation. The certificates are the same all over England regardless of county, although the examples here will focus on people from Dorset. Civil registration was introduced in England and Wales in July 1837. This means this source alone can help us trace back to the mid-1700s; for example, a burial record from 1837 may give a person's age as ninety meaning they were born around 1747, although the age is usually a rough estimate.

BMD certificates should always be sourced to confirm relationships between individuals. Most people have their own birth certificate and may be lucky enough to possess certificates belonging to their parents, grandparents or beyond. Where these are missing and where possible, these should be sought to ensure the correct lineage is researched.

It can help to become familiar with the registration districts so it is easier to find the relevant record from the GRO Index. Districts have changed over time; for example, the registration district of Weymouth was in use until 1 Apr 1997, when it merged to become part of the South Dorset registration district.

Knowing the local area or having a look at a map can help you to understand which district is most likely to feature your ancestor. On the whole, the historic registration districts for Dorset are Beaminster, Blandford, Bridport, Dorchester, Poole, Shaftesbury, Sherborne, Sturminster, Wareham, Weymouth, Wimborne and Wincanton.

Locating the Record

While many subscription genealogy sites offer a certificate purchasing service, it is much cheaper and quicker to buy certificates directly from the General Registration Office (GRO). By visiting www.gro.gov.uk you can view their online indexes for births and deaths which give basic information. This is free! For births, the index gives the child's name, the three-month (quarterly) period in which they were registered, where the birth was registered and the mother's maiden name. For deaths, the index again gives the person's name, the three-month (quarterly) period when the death was registered, the place the death and the age at death.

GRO References may appear confusing at first but once you break these down into sections they are simple to decipher. They begin with the year of the event followed by the quarter in which the event was registered. The quarters each contain three months:

- Quarter 1 (M) – Jan/Feb/Mar
- Quarter 2 (J) – Apr/May/Jun
- Quarter 3 (S) – Jul/ Aug/Sep
- Quarter 4 (D) – Oct/Nov/Dec

This means if the quarter reference is 1, the event was registered between January and March of that year. This will show as 'M' quarter in the GRO online Index, after the last month in the quarter. Remember, an event may occur in December but is not registered until January the following year. The volume number and page number come next. For example, my grandmother Dorothy Jessie Taylor's GRO birth reference is <u>Weymouth 1917/4/05A/372</u>. This shows her birth was registered in the fourth quarter of 1917 in Weymouth, volume 05A, page 372. Her birth certificate confirms she was born in November. You cannot know this from viewing the index or reference alone.

The information supplied in the GRO index is usually enough to confirm the correct identification of a person, however, you may find two births for John Smith registered at the same time in the same area. If you are not sure of the mother's maiden name at this point, you might have to purchase both certificates to discover which relates to your ancestor.

When researching Dorset ancestry, it can often prove cheaper to pay for a subscription to the Ancestry website because they have uploaded images of various registrars' books, such as their collection Dorset Marriages and Banns 1813-1921. This shows the book entry for the marriage which contains the same information as a certificate from GRO. Always make sure you see the handwritten entry and never rely on a typed transcription, in case of any errors.

You may be lucky and find that relatives are happy to share BMD certificates with you that they have already purchased which reduces your costs. Where you need to order the certificates from GRO yourself, it is simple to fill in their online order form using the known details of the event.

One website worth checking out is the Dorset Death Certificate Index

2. Death certificate of 19-year-old Daisy Charlotte Spencer of Bincombe, naming her husband Charles, a farm carter.

(https://dorsetdci.com). This is a transcribed listing of over 1000 death certificates which have been handed to the website's owner, Mark Collyer. There is an easy to use search box into which you are advised to type a surname, but you can also search by parish name if you wish. The results will show you the full transcription of the death certificate which features that surname. The beauty of this website is that results will also include the informants whom are often relatives of the deceased. There is an opportunity for you to contribute to the project by sending in scans of your family's death certificates.

Values of the Record
BMD certificates are essential to prove identification. There are countless stories of people who have relied on family hearsay regarding parentage; some have even copied other people's online trees only to find after years of researching the wrong tree that a branch much further down was incorrect. Ordering just one certificate could save you a lot of time researching an incorrect line.

I was guilty of this myself when I first started my research many years ago and didn't know any better. I found a family in the census; my great-grandmother Sophia, living with people whom I assumed were her parents as she was listed as 'daughter' along with her siblings. I researched trees of both parents for about a year before ordering her birth certificate. It turned out she had a different mother who died after she was born. Her father had then remarried and produced her half-siblings with his new wife who appeared in the census. It is a common mistake to make and whilst it is not one to be ashamed of, it is certainly one that needs admitting to so that the error can be corrected.

Looking in turn at each of the available certificates shows their usefulness. The information below shows the information given in each certificate.

Birth Certificate
- Registration district and sub-district
- County
- Date of birth
- Place of birth
- Child's name
- Child's sex
- Father's name
- Mother's name (including maiden name)
- Father's occupation
- Informant's name, residence and relationship
- Date of registration
- Registrar's signature

Marriage Certificate
- Place of marriage (venue and parish)
- County
- Date of marriage ceremony
- Names of the bride and groom
- Bride and groom's ages (often noted as 'full age')
- Marital status (i.e. whether divorced or widowed)
- Bride and groom's occupations
- Bride and groom's residences
- Bride and groom's fathers' names and occupations
- Whether married by banns or licence
- Signature of bride and groom (Or 'X' if illiterate)
- Signatures of at least two witnesses

Death Certificate
- Registration district and sub-district
- County
- Date of death
- Place of death
- Name of deceased
- Sex of deceased
- Age of deceased
- Occupation of deceased
- Cause of death
- Informant's name, residence and relationship
- Date of registration
- Registrar's signature

Generally speaking, the more recent the record, the more information it is likely to give. For example, where a person's residence is written, you are more likely to find an address in recent records. In older records closer to 1837, it will usually just state their parish. Cause of death is also likely to be more accurate if the record is more recent, whereas many older certificates just state *visitation by God, natural causes* or *old age* - none of which provide us with the most useful information.

Using subscription genealogy websites, it is possible to search for a child born into a marriage by typing in their father's surname, mother's surname, rough year of birth and county of birth. Using a wide enough variety of dates, the search results should show all of the children born into that marriage from mid-1837 onwards. In some cases, it is the child's birth certificate which is found first, showing their mother's maiden name. This can then be used in a similar way to search for the marriage between the child's parents.

If your ancestor was born before civil registration but they have younger siblings born after July 1837, it is worth purchasing their sibling's birth certificates to see what information these hold. Similarly, if your ancestor has a common name, such as Simon Smith, and you are unsure which birth certificate relates to your ancestor, then consider purchasing their sibling's birth certificates first if their name is less common, such as Zilpah Smith. Once you have discovered their mother's maiden name, it should then be easier to find the correct Simon Smith's birth certificate from the index.

Limitations of the Record

The researcher should be aware that neither the GRO indexes nor the certificates themselves are guaranteed to be completely reliable. For example, my second great-grandmother, Elizabeth Osment, is incorrectly recorded as 'Elizabeth Osmint'. When searching for an exact spelling match in the index she will not appear. Therefore, it is always recommended to search with the 'similar sounding variations' option on the website to ensure your ancestor is not missed.

When Born.	Name, if any.	Sex.	Name and Surname of Father.	Name and Maiden Surname of Mother.	Rank or Profession of Father.	Signature, Description, and Residence of Informant.
Nineteenth January 1861 Preston	Elizabeth	Girl	Thomas Osmint	Elizabeth Osmint formerly Read	Railway Labourer	+ The Mark of Elizabeth Osmint Mother Preston

3. Birth certificate of Elizabeth 'Osmint'.

There are also many cases where a father's name is not given on a birth certificate, implying the mother was unmarried when the child was born. There are many options in this case as to possible explanations, such as the baby's parents may have married after the birth, the mother may not have known who the father was or they simply failed to continue the relationship. Paternity can be hard to trace in these cases, especially more recent cases where some records are kept confidential for 100 years.

There are other cases where the father's name given on a birth certificate is incorrect. This can happen on any record as people have always, and will always, lie sometimes to protect themselves or a family secret. A married woman who has had a secret affair may see no reason to come clean and will simply list her husband as the father, with both men involved unaware of the true parentage. Similarly, a father's name given on a marriage certificate may also be incorrect. This happened with one of my ancestors who was adopted but gave a false father's name to hide the fact that he did not know who his father was.

My great-grandfather, Ernest Taylor, was a trigamist - married to three women at the same time! Whilst this is not common, you may find people lying about their marital status, claiming to be single or widowed so that they could marry again without needing a divorce. In Ernest's case he claimed he was a widower for his second marriage and a bachelor for his third.

Despite this, records of civil registration are amongst some of the more reliable records. Whilst it can be time-consuming and expensive to collect them all, it is necessary to be confident with your research going ahead.

Dorset Examples

Looking at how civil registration can help with Dorset ancestry, I have chosen my second great-grandmother, Elizabeth Osment, as an example. As mentioned before, her birth entry in the GRO Index incorrectly gives her name as Elizabeth Osmint. On viewing her birth certificate, it shows she was born on the 19 Jan 1861 at Preston to parents Thomas Osment, a railway labourer, and Elizabeth (née Read). Her mother was the informant who registered the birth on 7 Feb 1861.

4. Marriage certificate of Walter Eli Hatcher and Elizabeth Osment.

Elizabeth's marriage features in the Ancestry collection, meaning the certificate did not need to be purchased. This shows that Elizabeth was aged twenty when she married Walter Eli Hatcher, aged twenty-one at Preston, Dorset in 1881. They were both previously unmarried. Elizabeth was residing at Sutton Poyntz and Walter came from Osmington. They have both signed the record, along with witnesses Charles and Hannah Osment. In this example, the witnesses are both siblings of Elizabeth. The relationship is not given for witnesses, however, it is common that they are related and it is always worth looking into this.

Elizabeth's death certificate shows she died in Broadmayne on 30 Jul 1945, just three days before the end of World War II. She is correctly described as being eighty-four years of age and the widow of Walter. Her cause of death is simply described as *senility* and it was registered by her daughter, my great-grandmother, Susan Eunice Quinton, on 1 Aug.

Looking at the three BMD certificates for Elizabeth gives us a good outline of her life, and when all three have been found we shall know within which dates we can search other records to find her. Civil registration certificates give us crucial dates and relationships, but to find out more about the person as an individual it is necessary to look for other sources.

CHAPTER 2
Censuses

About the Record

The census returns of 1841-1921 are often the first records that family historians come across and also amongst the easiest to access and understand. UK censuses were also taken every ten years between 1801 and 1831. These early ones seldom survive and it is rare to find people named, with the records usually consisting of not much more than a parish headcount.

Notable early censuses that survive for Dorset are Winterborne St Martin, Melbury Osmond, Sturminster Newton and Oborne in 1801, Whitchurch Canonicorum and Corfe Castle in 1811, Compton Abbas, Corfe Castle, Marnhull, Horton, Thornford, Winterborne Whitechurch, Woodlands and Shaftesbury in 1821 and Allington, Corfe Castle and Ryme Intrinseca in 1831. Most name the head of the household, their occupation and state how many males and females resided in the house. Others are more detailed, such as the 1801 Oborne census which lists everybody within the parish and their marital status, with an occupation given for the head of the household.

There are many unique censuses taken prior to 1801, often for reasons of local provision. These include a numerical census of Marnhull in 1741 and the 1790 census of Corfe Castle and the surrounding area, including Kingston. The latter is particularly detailed, giving the full name, age, occupation, income and marital status of everyone in the parish. A minority of those listed also have their relationships listed, such as thirteen-year-old Elizabeth Baker, named as the granddaughter of seventy-two-year-old Mary Trim in Kingston. Elizabeth is stated to be a flax spinner with an income of two shillings.

The census returns that are most commonly used are those from 1841 onwards. From this date, the records show every person named within a household with their ages and occupations. From 1851 their birth place and relationship to the head of the household is given. Most frequently, there is a male head of the household with his wife and their children but other relationships are also found such as grandchildren, cousins and nieces and nephews.

The more recent the census record, the more likely you are to find more detail. The 1841 census is particularly stingy with information with only one occupation allowed to be noted per person and the birth place information limited to a question asking if the person was born in the same county that they were residing – yes or no! From 1851 specific birth places could be named and over time these became more specific, particularly if a person was born abroad.

In order to know which of your ancestors will appear in a particular census return, it helps to know on which date the census was taken.

- 1841   6 June
- 1851   30 March
- 1861   7 April
- 1871   2 April
- 1881   3 April
- 1891   5 April
- 1901   31 March
- 1911   2 April
- 1921   19 June

When using the census, the best method to search for ancestors is to work backwards, starting with the most recent record in which they feature. So for an ancestor who died in 1865, you should start with their appearance in the 1861 census before finding them in the 1851 and 1841 census. This helps to track changes in their household and marital status.

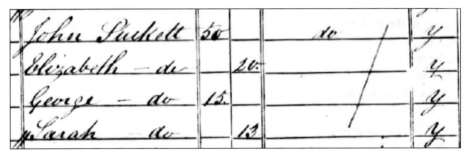

5. *1841 Census extract showing John, Elizabeth, George and Sarah Puckett in Sutton Poyntz.*

Locating the Record

Census returns are best accessed online at all subscription genealogy websites, such as Ancestry, FindMyPast, MyHeritage and The Genealogist. At the time of publication, the 1921 census is currently only available from FindMyPast, but this will be opened up to other sites at a later date. The original census records are held at The National Archives.

In order to find your ancestor in the census, use the search function on the website and enter the details that you know about them. It is often best to ensure you are not searching for the 'exact' search terms. For example, people may be recorded by their middle name, their age may be incorrectly transcribed or their birth place may be written as a county rather than a particular parish.

For some people, locating an ancestor in the census is easy. As popular genealogy television programmes often show, it is as simple as entering the information and one correct entry appears. This isn't always true; a correct entry first time is lucky but unusual, so great care needs to be taken to ensure the right person is found. Accepting just one wrong census entry can lead you down the wrong path researching the mistaken family for generations.

As with all records, looking for a person with a common name is usually the hardest. Searching for an Elizabeth Smith in Dorset in 1861 brings up seventy-three results. So what's the best way of ensuring you're researching the right person? Sometimes you will be lucky and there will only be one person at a specific address. Narrowing the results of Elizabeth Smith down to those born in Whitchurch Canonicorum leaves only two options - one born in 1833 and the other born in 1855. You can do the same by restricting your age options. A notable occupation can also help with identification. Someone with a common name may also live with someone with a less common first name, such as their spouse or child, so it may be easier to locate them first.

For census listings prior to 1841, check for transcribed records at Dorset OPC (www.opcdorset.org). A majority of these original records held at Dorset History Centre.

Values of the Record

One of the best things about census returns is that people of all ages and backgrounds feature in them, and from 1851 relationships are stated too. Many other records do not feature women, children or the poor but the census thankfully records all these groups. With the records taken every ten years, they can help us to form a picture of changing home lives and can lead us to discover ancestors' births, baptisms, deaths and burial records according to when they appear and disappear from the census.

Census returns are particularly helpful in tracing an ancestor's location and their birth place. Your family may have resided in the same village for hundreds of years, or you may be surprised to discover that they lived in a different parish in each census. Whatever the case, it is extremely useful to be able to know where the family was living at a point in time so you can locate them in other sources, including parish registers, title deeds and newspaper records.

6. *1881 Census extract showing married couple Thomas and Elizabeth Osment with their children Sarah, Charles and Frederick. Ages and occupations are given.*

The amount of detail provided in each census is also a huge bonus to the researcher. Whilst other records, such as tax lists or oath returns may simply give a person's name and parish, the information given in the census can help us positively identify a person and distinguish them from others with the same name.

Extra details you may find include your ancestor's employer being named in the 1921 census and the number of children born to a married couple and whether they are still alive in the 1911 census.

Census returns taken prior to 1841 are of great value, especially as these were taken prior to civil registration. They can therefore help you to locate your ancestors in parish registers, as well as giving a unique insight into a household.

Limitations of the Record
Contrary to popular belief, not everybody will be found in each census return. Some people purposefully hid from the census enumerators who came to collect details, perhaps due to suspicion of why their details were being collected or because they had a criminal past. Many suffragettes refused to complete their 1911 census as a protest. Others were simply missed through human error of the enumerators who missed certain houses or failed to take the details of travelling communities. Other records have unfortunately been lost. In the case of Dorset, this is most noticeable for 1851 where the parishes below suffered a partial loss of records:

- Bagber
- Child Okeford
- Hammoon
- Hinton St Mary
- Manston
- Okeford Fitzpaine
- Stoke Wake
- Sturminster Newton
- Belchalwell
- Fifehead Neville
- Hazelbury Bryan
- Ibberton
- Shillingstone
- Woolland

Nevertheless, a majority of people will be found. If you are struggling to locate an ancestor, there are a number of possibilities to consider. People can be recorded under their middle name, or even a nickname and birth places and ages are often not consistent throughout the census returns either. Just because your ancestor was twenty in 1861 does *not* mean he will necessarily be found aged ten in 1851.

There are numerous transcription errors that have been made too and this makes finding the correct person more difficult. These mistakes sometimes happened at the point of collection where a census enumerator misheard a birth place for example and so recorded this wrongly. It is more common to find transcription errors online where a person has misread or mistyped the information leading to inaccurate search results. Different subscription websites have used different people for their transcriptions meaning one website may have the information correctly written, whereas another may bring up zero results. Therefore, where possible, it would make sense to search for a missing person using an alternative site.

When a person cannot be found, it is best to minimise the amount of information you use to search for them to try to avoid these errors hindering your research. For example, rather than searching specifically for a John Jones in Beaminster aged fifty-three who works as a blacksmith, try widening the search and look for a John Jones living within ten miles of Beaminster, aged between forty-five and sixty without an occupation. Our ancestors changed their occupations and moved parishes more often than you might think, so don't immediately rule out somebody who doesn't match the search terms exactly.

You should also bear in mind that in 1841 enumerators were instructed to round the ages down to the nearest five of anyone aged over fifteen. This advice was not always followed, so you will still find some exact ages given, so bear in mind you will need to expand the age range when searching this census.

The stated relationships are not always accurate either with definitions of terms changing over time. For example, grandchildren were sometimes referred to as nieces and nephews and that totally confuses the issue! Also, never assume that, because a person is missing from the family household, they have died. They may be found in the workhouse, in prison or children may be staying with other relatives. The census noted where each person was on the particular night of recording, and this was *not* necessarily where they lived. If a person travelled for work, they may be found far from home.

Dorset Examples

The census can be useful to find anyone alive between 1841 and 1921. As people of all ages and backgrounds should feature, this is a fantastic record to give an insight into a person's changing family life.

My fourth great-grandmother, Mary Read (née Croad), was born in 1793 and died in 1865, meaning she features in three census returns for 1841, 1851 and 1861. In 1841 she is recorded as being aged forty-eight, living with William Read, known from parish registers to be her husband, aged fifty-eight and working as an agricultural labourer. Also present are their children Leah, Mary, Ellen and Amelia, aged nineteen, twelve, eight and five respectively, living together in Sutton Poyntz. The census states they were all born in Dorset.

Fast-forward to the 1851 census return and Mary is still living in Sutton Poyntz, this time aged fifty-eight, however, she is now described as a widow. She is living with her daughters Leah, Ellen and Amelia, aged twenty-nine, eighteen and fifteen and all four are noted as being born in Sutton Poyntz. Mary has no occupation listed.

Finding from this record that Mary is a widow helps to narrow down the dates of when to search for William's death. This is helpful given his common name. Records show William died in 1847.

By 1861 we see another chapter in Mary's changing life. She is now residing in neighbouring Preston, aged sixty-eight and is described as a pauper. She is living with her grandson, Peter Miller aged three months and a visitor named Emma Sargent, aged twenty-one. Researching the parish registers show that Peter is the daughter of Amelia Read, who sadly passed away shortly after his birth.

These census returns are examples of how they can reveal an ancestor's changing circumstances within their family life. In the space of twenty years, Mary went from being a married mother living with four children to a pauper widow caring for her three-month-old grandson. They are, however, a snapshot in time and should be used in conjunction with other sources to discover more. For example, in this case, parish registers show that Peter died soon after the census was taken, with Mary herself passing away in 1865.

7. The 1861 Census return showing a widowed Mary living with her grandson Peter and a visitor named Emma Sargent.

CHAPTER 3
Parish Registers

About the Record

Once you have traced your family back in time using the GRO and census records, the next records to take you back further generations are the parish registers - these record baptisms, marriages and burials within a parish. The amount of information you will find in these depends on the date that the record was written and who completed the register. Some clerks recorded extra details in their notes which can prove very helpful. Generally, the earlier in time the record was made, the least information it will give, often stating just a name and a burial date.

Not all parish registers have survived. Whilst all parishes were ordered to keep registers from 1538, it is rare to find a complete set from this time. Early records were kept on loose sheets of paper, many of which were lost. From 1597 the registers were required by law to be bound, meaning more survived after this date. After this date you may come across registers which are damaged or illegible. Those transcribing the records into the new parchment books in 1597 were requested to write in previous paper entries, although most stopped at 1558.

You may come across Bishops' Transcripts from 1597. Those for Dorset are held at Wiltshire & Swindon History Centre. These are copies of parish registers and can prove very helpful where the original parish register has been lost. Often abbreviated to BTs, the transcripts were sent to the bishop within one month of Easter every year. They sometimes contain extra details that aren't seen in the parish register so it is worth consulting both if possible. Sadly, the 1731 fire of Blandford Forum destroyed nearly all of the Bishops' Transcripts for the county that were deposited here, along with other parish records that were held in the church.

As new laws came into force, the essential details that were to be recorded in the registers increased. Hardwick's Marriage Act 1753 introduced a standardised format for entries of marriage for the first time. Baptism and burial records were not regulated until George Rose's Act 1812 when printed forms began to be used. Therefore, from these dates the information you can expect to find is more predictable, assuming they were filled out correctly.

8. Early parish registers were usually vague. This shows Stephen Squib and Mary Hoskins were married on 29 May 1743 at Preston church.

It is not unusual to find your ancestor in different parishes for each of their lifetime events. My sixth great-grandmother, Elizabeth 'Betty' Chipp, was baptised in Winterborne Steepleton, married in Little Bredy and was buried in Preston. Our ancestors often moved about more than we might think, so keep an open mind as to your forebears' possible movements around the county and beyond.

Locating the Record

Dorset parish registers are held at Dorset History Centre. They have all been digitised and are available online, currently at Ancestry. Check out the Dorset History Centre's webpage to see what parish registers and Bishop's Transcripts survive for the parish you are researching - www.dorsetcouncil.gov.uk/libraries-history-culture/dorset-history-centre/collections/parish-registers. You will find there are many free transcriptions available online, one of the best being at Dorset Online Parish Clerks website, often referred to as Dorset OPC (www.opcdorset.org). This is an excellent resource which is regularly updated and contains a wide array of transcribed Dorset records arranged by parish. This is a great place to easily browse the parish register entries. When you have found an entry relating to your family you can use the information to search for this original image on Ancestry. As with every record, it is best to check the original image for any transcription errors.

Carry on tracing your tree back in time using the registers. After finding the earliest record of a couple in the 1841 census, you can use their rough birth year and location from other census entries to try and find their marriage record. If they had children after 1837 the mother's maiden name can be found online on the GRO indexes (free to browse for births and deaths) or on the child's birth certificate. Searching for a marriage between the two people should bring up one or more possibilities for you. The correct marriage entry may be obvious - for example, they may have an unusual name or the witnesses may also be relatives. Sometimes a process of elimination is required to ensure you have the right entry. This may involve tracing the tree forward of both married couples to see which matches with your tree.

When you have found their marriage date, you should then check the baptism registers for the years after this for any children born prior to 1837 as you would not have a birth certificate for them. Most couples will have their first child within two years of their marriage. At this point check the burial registers too as some of their children may have died before reaching adulthood. In this case, the names of the parents are often recorded alongside the child's name.

FreeREG (www.freereg.org.uk) is a free transcription site giving free access to parish register entries, provided by volunteers. Results can be broken down by county and by parish, with the number of transcriptions available varying. Abbotsbury has over 5,000 entries, Gillingham has just under 1000 entries, but

Lytchett Minster has just forty results. Some parishes have no records at all. It is also worth checking on Family Search (www.familysearch.org). Like FreeREG, this is a free service that only provides transcriptions.

Using parish registers for genealogical research often means darting about between baptism, marriage and burial records for multiple parishes to ensure you are researching the correct family and have gathered as much information as possible. Try to do so in a logical manner and make a note of which registers you have viewed for which dates and for which surname to keep a track of your research.

Values of the Record

Before the implementation of birth, marriage and death registration in 1837, parish registers are usually the only evidence you will find of baptism, marriage and burial. They are a fantastic resource which in some cases can take your tree back to the sixteenth century. Many have extra details added in by the informant, such as date of birth or age at death - before it was legally required. In rare cases you may find additional information such as a cause of death considered significant, perhaps death caused by drowning or even murder.

The value of the record depends on the year of the event and how much information the registrar was required to record. Hardwicke's Marriage Act 1753 aimed to discourage irregular marriages and there were a number of new marriage regulations - the marriage had to take place in the parish of residence of either the bride or groom and the marriage had to be by licence or by banns which were read three times in the weeks preceding the marriage. Quakers were exempt but other nonconformist groups found themselves having to marry in their parish church rather than their own chapel in order for the marriage to be legally recognised. When it comes to documentation, there was a new banns book to be completed and a marriage register. Both were printed and then the details completed by hand.

9. The 1781 marriage of John Read and Susannah Slade at Preston showing the standardised format introduced in 1754.

From 1754, the information that was to be completed in the new marriage register comprised of the following - bride and groom's name, their residence, marital status, their signature or mark, whether the marriage was by banns or licence, signatures of witnesses and the name of the officiating minister. This is a vast improvement giving us much more information that we can use, because previously, entries in the parish register for marriages may have only noted the couple's name and the date that they married. The names of the witnesses may prove crucial if they are relatives. Whether your ancestor signed their name or left their mark, usually an 'X', can tell you if they were literate or not; some people were able to write their name but nothing else. If they married by banns you should be able to find them in the banns register, although the only extra information this will tell you is on what three dates the banns were read. Having the bride and groom's residence at the time of their marriage is a big help and can help you find their baptism if they were born there. You may find other records relating to this residence too including apprenticeship and court records.

Baptisms and burials were not standardised until 1812, meaning before this date you may find minimal information in parish registers. George Rose's Act of that year instructed parishes to record baptisms and burials on a prescribed printed form and this then gave much more detail in the entries. The printed pages consist of a table with a new entry for each row. The baptism register entries contain the child's name, the parents' names, their residence, the father's occupation and the officiating minister's name. The residence is often just the name of the village where they lived but may give a more precise location. By tracing the baptisms of your ancestors' siblings, you can track changes in residence and father's occupation.

The burial register entries from 1812 onwards contain the deceased's name, their age, residence and the officiating minister's name. The residence again takes the same format as baptisms and the age given for the deceased is often just an estimate. This can be used to help find their baptism, but remember that the informant at the burial may not be exactly sure how old their deceased relative was.

When Baptized.	Child's Christian Name.	Parents Name.		Abode.	Quality, Trade, or Profession.	By whom the Ceremony was performed.
		Christian.	Surname.			
1831. Feb 13th No. 1369.	Ellen	William and Elizabeth	Read	Gillingham	Blacksmith	David Read

10. *The format of baptism registers from 1812.*
This shows the baptism of Ellen Read in Gillingham in 1831.

People were not even as certain about their own ages as we are today, largely due to the lack of official documentation that is so familiar to us now.

If you have any nonconformists in your family tree, they may still appear in parish registers. From 1754, nonconformists will be found in the marriage registers, although some chose to have a second ceremony in their own chapel of choice. They are likely to have been buried within the parish church cemetery if their chapel did not have its own grounds. Sometimes the registers note that they are, for example, *Catholic*, and these ceremonies often happened at night. An adult baptism in the parish register may hint that the person previously belonged to a nonconformist family but wished to return to the Church of England. You can read more in the Nonconformists chapter in this book.

Name.	Abode.	When buried.	Age.	By whom the Ceremony was performed.
Richard Pearcy No. 537.	Affpuddle	Jany 6th	77	H Williams Julian view

11. The layout of a burial register from 1812 onwards.
This shows the burial of Richard Pearcy in Affpuddle in 1881.

Limitations of the Record

Never assume that a tenuous link may belong to your ancestor just because the names match and it appears to be the only possibility. Say for example that you are looking for a baptism entry for Benjamin Penny born around 1710 in Sixpenny Handley. You may discover that there is only one match for that name within a ten-year time frame in Dorset – but it is at Beaminster. Someone may assume that this must mean it is their ancestor and that they had moved some forty miles away across the county. What is more likely is that Benjamin was born in or around Sixpenny Handley (even possibly in nearby Wiltshire) but the records have not survived. The registers for Beaminster survive back to 1585, but Sixpenny Handley's earliest entry only dates from 1754. Always find out which parish registers have survived for your parish of interest and from which date.

Families moved around more often than you think. You may find a branch that resided in the same village for generations, or discover that each generation moved to a nearby parish, seemingly hopping around the county or further afield. It can be hard and sometimes impossible to trace your family through parish registers alone *and* still be confident that you are tracing the right people! The best way of being sure is to view the registers for nearby parishes to see if the surname can be seen there at the same time. Don't forget to correspond with other records to back up your findings, such as through probate and court records.

The number of parish registers that have been lost or are now illegible is a limitation, and if the record cannot be found in Bishop's Transcripts either, then a record of that event is unlikely to be found elsewhere. Many parish registers were not completed during the Period of Commonwealth (1641-1660) which explains gaps at this time. Many chose to baptise their children after the Restoration of 1660, so be aware that those baptised in 1660 and 1661 could be 'older' children rather than infants, compared with other years when it is usually babies who are baptised.

Between 1694 and 1706 there was a tax on births, marriages and burials; this meant some people chose not to baptise their children during this time to avoid paying the tax. Paupers were exempt so will still be found, as well as those happy to pay the tax. There was another tax between 1783 and 1794 when the Stamp Act enforced a 3d fee on every entry in the parish register. As with the earlier tax there was much disapproval of this.

Dorset Examples

A majority of parish register entries will follow the expected format for that period. In other cases there will be extra detail. Looking at the parish register for Caleb Angel, my seventh great-grandfather, in Osmington, we can see he was baptised on 6 Apr 1716 as an adult prior to his marriage. This is a rare occurrence to find within Church of England parish registers. Caleb married at Winterborne Came the following month on 2 May 1716 to Elizabeth Cake. He was buried in Osmington on 16 Nov 1774 where it is noted he was *aged 90 years*. A majority of entries in this register state basic facts of names and dates, however, any significant details have been noted by the informant, such as in this case where Caleb reached a very old age for that time. On the previous page it is noted that Daniel Winser and his wife Elizabeth were buried in the same grave on 12 May 1772. Osmington parish registers start from 1691 meaning any earlier reference to Caleb or his Angel family before this time cannot be found here.

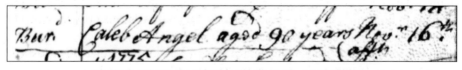

12. The burial entry for Caleb Angel in Osmington parish registers.

An earlier example in the Swanage parish registers shows that Henry Tarry, my eleventh great-grandfather, was baptised on 11 Jun 1617, listed as the son of Henry. No mother's name is given. The writing in this register is harder to read but most is still legible with time and patience. Unfortunately, there are two entries on the page which are unreadable due to a large stain in the centre of the page.

CHAPTER 4
Other Parish Records

About the Record

Most people researching their family tree will come across parish registers fairly early on in their research but there other records to consider; these are less well known but are equally as useful to genealogists. They are wonderfully varied including bastardy documentation, records of settlement and removal, parish official meeting minutes and workhouse registers. Parish records cover everyone within the parish and are a great source of information for our poorer ancestors who do not appear in other records, such as tax listings.

There are many parish records relating to the giving and receiving of poor relief within the parish. The Poor Relief Act of 1662, also known as the Settlement Act, stated that a person or family must have a legal right of settlement in the parish to qualify for the receipt of poor relief from them. This right was usually assumed according to where a person was born or if a woman married a man who resided there. Settlement could also be gained in other ways, such as if a person served a seven-year apprenticeship within the parish, worked for over a year in the parish or lived there for over forty days without raising a complaint.

Parishes were in charge of raising their own poor relief funds from the residents, with the names of those who contributed often surviving in poor rate books. Parishes did not want to pay this poor relief to those who were not entitled to it and were not legal residents there. Some cases were clear-cut and a family who were known to have been born and married in a parish could receive poor relief without needing to be examined further. From 1697, settlement certificates were issued. These may name one person or a whole family and they were used as proof of their parish of settlement. This meant that they could move between parishes, perhaps to find work, but if they needed to claim poor relief they would return to claim this from their legal settlement.

If the parish doubted a person's or a family's legal settlement there, then Justices of the Peace could undertake an enquiry. These settlement examinations are often fantastically detailed and they can give a person's place of birth, place of apprenticeship and work, names of family members and within which parishes they have lived and for how long. Their reliability needs to be questioned when people are recalling certain details from many years previously or where they may be lying in order to gain settlement in a particular place. These details were then used by

Justices of the Peace to decide what the person's place of settlement was and where they had the right to claim poor relief.

If the Justices of the Peace decided that a person or family had no right to settlement in their parish, then a removal order could be issued. These documents name the person or persons to be removed, the parish they were being removed from and the parish they were being relocated to. The person or family were then escorted to the parish boundary and handed over from one constable to another. The Poor Removal Act of 1795 stopped parishes from removing people until they actually claimed poor relief.

Children born to unwed mothers were of particular concern to parish officials because they were likely to become chargeable to the parish. Officials undertook bastardy examinations in an attempt to establish who the father of the child was, so that he could pay for its upbringing. In these examinations, the mother named the 'reputed father' and the sex of the child is given, unfortunately without a name. A bastardy bond was then issued, whereby the father swore to contribute to the child's costs. If a man refused to pay, he could be imprisoned. Sometimes the father is not known or cannot be found and in these cases another person may be named in the bond, such as the grandparent of the child, who can pay child maintenance.

From 1601, overseers of the parish could arrange apprenticeships for pauper children in their care; these were often illegitimate children. This removed the need for the parish to pay for their relief, with the child's master paying for their housing and food in return for training them in their trade. The apprenticeship was usually for seven years, although many were not completed and were often undertaken in a different parish to that of their legal settlement. Apprentices were often treated badly, being abused and over-worked, so many fled. Other apprenticeships ceased when the master moved or died. There are many examples in Quarter Sessions records relating to pauper apprenticeships failing, whether due to the fault of the apprentice or the master.

Parish officials kept written records relating to their accounts and the work they had undertaken within the area. The running of the parish was done by the vestry, a group of parishioners who held regular meetings when minutes were made. Churchwarden's accounts list money spent on furnishing the church and repairs as well as other related outgoings, such as paying bell-ringers.

Overseer's account books give the names of people receiving poor relief, whether this was on a regular basis or as a one-off payment. Surveyors of the Highways, otherwise known as *waywardens*, kept accounts relating to the building and repairing of highways in the parish and sometimes named those carrying out the manual labour, along with how much they were paid. Constable's accounts name petty criminals and people who were removed from the parish.

Parishes established workhouses from the late 1600s to care for the sick poor

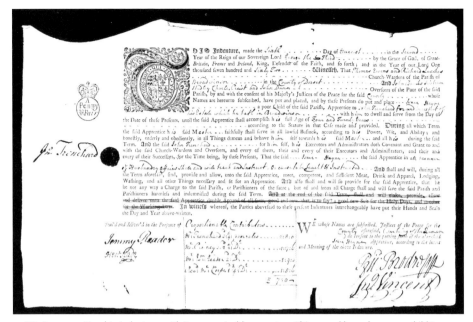

13. *An apprenticeship indenture with its recognisable wavy top. This record bounds pauper child Isaac Hayne to John Trenchard of Broadwindsor.*

of the parish and provide work for those who were able to do so. After the Poor Law Amendment Act of 1834, parishes were arranged into unions and union workhouses emerged. Surviving workhouse records include admission and discharge registers, punishment books, building plans, vaccination lists and accounts. Some of our ancestors may have entered the workhouse at some point in their life, with many having to live out their last days there.

Locating the Records

A majority of parish records are held at county record offices. Dorset History Centre holds a large collection of parish records, with many having been scanned, transcribed and available on Ancestry. Some collections survive much better than others. Unfortunately, few Dorset workhouse records have survived, with the most common surviving record being the minutes of the Board of Guardians which rarely give individuals names. These include the Guardians' minute books for Dorchester dating 1900-1930 and for Poole dating 1835-1930. Other surviving workhouse records include Blandford's register of inmates dating 1761-1765 and Beaminster's pauper offence book dating 1842-1869. Some Poor Law Union correspondence is held at The National Archives in MH 12. The website www.workhouses.org.uk lists what records survive for each workhouse and where to find them.

Due to the nature of some of the records, you may find your ancestor's parish records in another county record office. For example, if your ancestor was born in Dorset but then moved to a parish in Devon and tried to claim poor relief there, their settlement examination will be found at Devon Archives. The best way to find such records is to search The National Archives Discovery catalogue for your ancestor's name followed by 'Dorset' or their parish of birth. Examples include a 1770 examination for Edith Collins who was born at Folke but whose record is found at Devon Archives and a 1724 examination for Robert Turner who was born in Shaftesbury but whose record is held at Bedfordshire Archives.

Values of the Record

Settlement examinations can give a lot of information regarding where the person was born, where they married and where they lived and worked. Even where a short amount of detail is given, this is often enough to give you a new lead of where to trace them in other parishes records and registers. Ages of adults and children are sometimes given. As settlement examinations and removal orders name more than one parish, this record may be key to tracing an ancestor who goes missing from a certain parish register.

Bastardy records may provide you with the name of your ancestor's father, enabling you to trace a new branch of your tree. When an illegitimate child is baptised, the name of the father is rarely given and many assume this to be a dead end. Dorset has excellent surviving bastardy records available and you may find an examination, a bond or both to give you the name of the father and his parish of residence. Whilst the child is rarely named, their gender and date of birth are usually given.

Apprenticeship indentures arranged by the parish for pauper children can explain why the child's parish of settlement changed and the trade for which they trained. The child's father is often named and sometimes the child's birth place is given. The master is also named so this document is useful for people researching his history as well because it tells you where he was working and that he took on

14. *Bastardy record naming James Satchell of Charminster as the reputed father of Ann Minterne's child.*

an apprentice. Apprenticeships were often noted in vestry minutes and overseers' accounts.

Workhouse admission and discharge registers can tell you when a person entered and left the workhouse and it is noted if they died there, along with their date of death. Sometimes whole families entered the workhouse together. Other details may include their marital status, religion, occupation and parish of residence.

Parish records can give us an idea as to the issues our ancestors faced within their parish. If they were regular receivers of poor relief they would have had low standards of living. Surviving overseers' account books may tell you what items of clothing were donated to them, as well as any fuel or food. Knowing that your ancestor entered the workhouse can be particularly poignant, with this generally being a last resort for a family. The accounts of the parish officials can give an overall view of life within the parish, such as the vestry minutes and constables' accounts.

Some parish records are helpful simply to place a particular ancestor in the parish and a date and to know they were alive at this time; for example a person may be named in the churchwarden accounts, having been paid for carpentry work. Having an ancestor named in the overseers' poor rate books tells us that they were not deemed to be 'poor' and were contributing to the local rates. The records are also fascinating if your ancestor worked as a parish official, such as a constable or as a Justice of the Peace. Being able to see a large amount of evidence of their work and writing is of a huge interest and you can get a real sense of what they encountered day-to-day.

Limitations of the Record
It helps to understand which relatives you are more likely to find in each parish record. A person's settlement was generally questioned if they claimed poor relief so wealthier relatives will not feature in settlement examinations. However, they will feature in poor rate books, whereas paupers will not as they were exempt from paying. Frustratingly, names are not always given in records of the parish officials. For example, a constable's account may either say 'James Middleton removed' or simply 'poor man removed'.

The context of many of these records may not be clear. You may discover that your ancestor was a pauper receiving poor relief but you may not be able to find out why they needed to claim. This was often down to ill health but could be down to other factors such as if their house was lost in a fire or if they lost their employment. Settlement examinations may tell you that your ancestor moved regularly between numerous parishes but again the reasoning may not be clear. Apprenticeship indentures alone can also not confirm whether the full apprenticeship term was completed.

The reliability of the information provided in settlement examinations should be questioned. In some cases the information can lead to other records which can prove that they were truthful. For example, if the parish where they served their apprenticeship is given, then this may be proven through surviving apprenticeship records. Likewise if their place of birth is given, then this may be proven through baptism registers. It may be hard to prove if they resided in a named parish if no records survive from that area for that period.

The reliability of bastardy records is also uncertain. Parishes were under pressure to discover the father of a bastard child so that the parish would not have to pay for the child. Just because a man is listed as being the 'reputed father' in a bastardy document is certainly not concrete evidence that he did father the child. It can never be known what percentage of these named fathers was accurate, so where possible double-check with other sources. This may involve checking the Quarter Sessions records to see if the man denied the mother's claims that he was the father and refused to pay, or you may be lucky, as I was, to have the father confirmed through DNA testing. See the example of John Puckett in the DNA chapter of this book.

Survival of parish records varies from parish to parish and from record to record. Workhouse records from Dorset have not survived well. Whilst Dorset History Centre has done a superb job at cataloguing many records, including bastardy records and settlement examinations, other parish records are not yet indexed. For example, records such as constables' accounts and vestry minutes are not searchable by name and you will need to browse page by page to see if your ancestor features. Therefore, if you search Dorset History Centre's catalogue for your ancestor's name and no results are returned, it may just be that the names of the records that they do feature in have not yet been transcribed onto the catalogue.

Dorset Examples
My husband's sixth great-grandmother, Elizabeth Gillingham Sexey, was born illegitimately to parents John Gillingham and Elizabeth Sexey in Shitterton in 1733. Her baptism entry simply gives her name, her mother's name and her date of baptism. Looking further at the parish records gives a more comprehensive account of her coming to being. A settlement examination from June 1733 details how her mother was in the employment of John at the time of conception, working as his servant. After the birth of her illegitimate daughter, Elizabeth, she was ordered to be removed from Bere Regis back to Broadmayne, her last legal place of settlement, as noted in a removal order dated 27 Oct 1733. There is also a surviving bastardy order, which unusually names the child by her full name. John is noted to be a 'gentleman', living on his own means, so would have had no trouble in paying for his daughter's maintenance.

In a sad but not uncommon case of history repeating itself, Elizabeth Gillingham

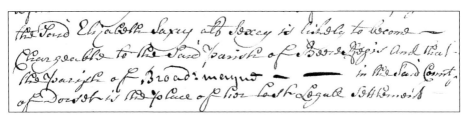

15. *Excerpt from Elizabeth Sexey's removal order dated 1733.*

Sexey went on to share a similar fate to her mother. In 1757, aged twenty-four, Elizabeth is seen in the baptism registers as an unwed mother to a son named William Moor Gillingham. A removal order dating 23 Apr 1757 shows she was removed from the parish of Tincleton shortly before William's birth, ironically to Bere Regis where her mother had previously wanted to reside. The bastardy order for her son names William Moor of Devon as the father. It was common for illegitimate children to be named after their fathers. Elizabeth went on to have another illegitimate child, this time a daughter named Betty, in 1767. The child's father is named as Robert Amey in the bastardy papers. All parish records used in this case are available to view on Ancestry.

CHAPTER 5

Wills and Probate

About the Record

The discovery of the will of an ancestor can be a hugely significant as they are full of genealogical information. At times it may be the only document proving a relationship between two family members thus enabling you to research back another generation in your tree. A will details a person's wishes regarding the people to whom they want their property and money to be left to after their decease. They may simply leave everything to a spouse or to one child or, if you're lucky, they will name a wide array of family members such as siblings, nieces and nephews. Other probate records include letters of administration (known as admons) found if a person died without a will, known as intestate. Inventories may also be found listing a person's belongings in an itemised manner. It is not guaranteed that a will, admons or an inventory will be found for each of your ancestors.

Strictly speaking, a will bequeathed realty (buildings and land) whereas a testament bestowed the deceased's personal property. This is why the documents together are known as the *will and testament* as they are found written in the same piece of text. Today most people simply refer to the documents as wills, despite them containing instructions for how to bequeath personal property.

Until 1883, a wife's property became her husband's upon marriage. This means anything that formerly belonged to her was now his to leave in a will, so you are unlikely to find a will for a married woman as technically she had nothing to leave to anybody. You will still find wills from single women and widows and these can prove very useful, leaving possessions to children and more distant relations. As well as relatives, you may find an ancestor has left their belongings to a friend or colleague which can also be of interest. You may find people bequeathing their homes, occupational buildings, clothes, jewellery, furniture, heirlooms and, of course, money. Some wills are short and vague in detail proving to be less helpful whereas others can be several pages long going into great detail about their belongings and wealth. You are less likely to find a will if your ancestor was poor. They had very little to leave and may have simply left instructions to their widow and children as to what should happen upon their death.

The Court of Probate Act 1857 led to a big change with regards to probate jurisdiction. This means that searching for an ancestor's will pre-1858 and post-1858 is very different – all due to the rule changes in the 1857 Act.

Locating the Record Pre-1858

Finding probate records prior to 1858 is unfortunately not straightforward. Depending on where the deceased owned property, their will could have been proved at a number of different ecclesiastical courts. For Dorset ancestors this could be Dorset Archdeaconry Court, Bristol Consistory Court, Peculiar Courts or the Prerogative Court of Canterbury (PCC). Wiltshire and Swindon Record Office hold probate records that were proved by the court of the Dean of Salisbury.

To locate a will proved prior to 1858, first establish when your ancestor died and within which parishes they owned realty or property. Parish maps available on Ancestry show their boundaries and helpfully note the probate jurisdiction for each area too. If your ancestor's property was within the jurisdiction of the same minor court then their will would be proved there. If your ancestor held realty which sat in two or more different jurisdictions, the will had to be proved in the higher court. Most Dorset parishes sat under Dorset Archdeaconry Court. These probate records are held at Dorset History Centre but have all been digitised and are available on Ancestry. Ensure you view all the relevant pages to your ancestor as it is easy to miss one.

If your ancestor's realty was held between two Archdeaconries within the same diocese, then the will was proved in a Consistory Court. In Dorset's case, they would be referred to Bristol Consistory Court. These wills are again held by Dorset History Centre but have again been digitised and are also available on Ancestry. Prior to 1542, Dorset was part of the Diocese of Salisbury.

If your ancestor bequeathed property that lay within two different dioceses then it would be proved by the PCC. This was the highest of the probate courts. Their probate record will also be held here if they died abroad, including soldiers, or if they held property abroad. The PCC was the only court allowed to prove wills during the Commonwealth period of 1653-1660. The PCC probate records are held at The National Archives with images of them available to view online at Ancestry and The Genealogist. At TNA, registered wills are held in PROB11, with inventories at PROB2-5 and administrations in PROB6-7.

The exceptions to the above rule are parishes that belonged to 'Peculiar' courts, of which there are quite a few in Dorset. Peculiars are outside the jurisdiction of the Archdeacon and/or the Bishop of the Diocese. People living within these Peculiars could have their wills proved in the relevant Peculiar Court, meaning they may be found at Wiltshire & Swindon History Centre or Dorset History Centre. A list of these is seen below along with what archives hold their original administrative documents.

Dorset History Centre
Peculiar of Canford Magna and Poole
Peculiar of Corfe Castle
Manor and Liberty of Frampton
Peculiar of Milton Abbas
Peculiar of Sturminster Marshall
Peculiar of Wimborne Minster

Wiltshire & Swindon History Centre
Prebendal Peculiar of Chardstock and Wambrook
Prebendal Peculiar of Fordington
Peculiar of Gillingham
Prebendal Peculiar of Lyme Regis and Halstock
Prebendal Peculiar of Netherbury
Prebendal Peculiar of Preston and Sutton Poyntz
Peculiar of the Dean of Salisbury
Peculiar of Wimborne Minster
Prebendal Peculiar of Yetminster

From this previous list, wills from the Peculiars allocated to Dorset History Centre are available on Ancestry. Confusingly, wills from many of the peculiars allocated to WSHC can be found at DHC and are therefore also online at Ancestry. Therefore it is still worth checking Ancestry for your ancestor's will first, before referring to WSHC for any related documentation.

These Peculiar courts are not limited to the parishes in their titles. For example, the Peculiar of Sturminster Marshall also covers Hamworthy, Lytchett Minster and Corfe Mullen. The other exceptions are the Manor and Liberty of Frampton which also covers Bettiscombe, Bincombe, Compton Valance and Winterborne Came, and the Peculiar of Milton Abbas which also covers Woolland. Durweston and Stourpaine are covered by the Dean and Chapter of Salisbury (held by Wiltshire & Swindon History Centre).

The Court of the Peculiar of the Dean of Salisbury had jurisdiction over the following Dorset parishes with records now held at held by Wiltshire & Swindon History Centre:

Alton Pancras	Beer Hackett
Bere Regis with Winterborne Kingston	Bloxworth
Castleton	Caundle Marsh
Charminster	Clifton Maybank
Folke	Haydon
Hermitage	Holnest

Kingston	Lillington
Longburton	Mapperton
Nether Compton	North Wootton
Oborne	Over Compton
Ryme Intrinseca	Sherborne
Stockwood	Stratton
Thornford	Turner's Puddle
Winterborne Anderson	Winterborne Tomson

Death duty was owed on estates over a set value from 1796-1903, with will abstracts being submitted to the Stamp Office. Indexes to Death Duty wills are available at TNA, Ancestry and FindMyPast. The indexes can tell you the deceased's date of death, brief details from the will and the executor's name. Today, the equivalent duty is known as inheritance tax.

16. *Extract from the Death Duty Index showing Betty Abbott's executor named as Isaac Abbott of Piddletrenthide.*

Locating the Record Post-1858

When locating a will, don't go searching exactly for the year that your ancestor died. Depending on how the record is catalogued, this may be by the date the will was written or when the will was proved, and a will may have been written several years *before* a person's death, sometimes decades. Alternatively a will may be proved several years after the person died. Search logically by name, place and date viewing the results in a sensible order of which is most likely to relate to your family. So how do you find a will for your ancestor?

In 1858 the Principal Probate Registry was established for wills created in England and Wales. Dorset copy wills from 1858 -1940 used to be held by the District Probate Registry at Blandford Forum but these have since been relocated to Dorset History Centre in Dorchester. These are not all complete copies and some are only summaries highlighting key points. As these summaries may miss other facts that are significant to your research, you should try to source the original. Dorset probate records from 1954 until today are held in Winchester at the Probate Registry.

When looking for a will post-1858, the easiest way to find this is by searching the National Probate Calendar online for free at https://probatesearch.service.gov.uk/. Select the correct tab regarding the date, which for genealogical purposes is most likely to be 'Wills and Probate 1858-1996'. Enter the surname and date of the person you are searching for and browse through the results to see if your ancestor is present. Unfortunately, at present there is no option for searching on the website by location, so if your ancestor has a common surname, it may take some time to find the right person. Remember, not everyone left a will, so don't be surprised if your ancestor isn't there.

When you have found your ancestor's entry, this will give a short summary including date of death, residence of the deceased, to whom probate was granted and sometimes their relationship. It also states where probate was granted and a value of the estate. At the bottom of the page is an option to order a copy of the will - this is advisable because you will gain more details about the deceased and their estate. It is unfortunately not possible to search by the name of the executor or beneficiaries, but if you happen to find your ancestor listed as one, purchasing the will could tell you how they knew the deceased. The wills are sent as a digital copy. Make sure you save them to your computer or other device and print them too. Letters of administration are found via the same website on the same search page.

Values of the Record

Different family members may be named in the will, often more so for an unmarried person (male or female) or a widow. The relationship between the deceased and the named person is usually stated but be aware that terms have changed over time; for example, a niece may be referred to as a cousin. From reading what a person has bequeathed, we can gain an understanding as to their financial situation and lifestyle. If a person has been left a small figure, such as one shilling, it can sometimes hint of ill feeling towards that person. If an eldest son is not mentioned, this is not unusual and probably because he might have already taken on the family business and therefore not be due anything else. Married daughters may also sometimes be omitted if they received a monetary figure upon marriage from their parents.

I have broken down brick walls in my tree by ordering a will on the off chance it may relate to my family. Taking a chance to order a will for a person in a particular parish with a rare surname, I have been lucky twice in discovering these wills have named many family members, proving a link between the deceased and my ancestors. This is obviously harder to do if your ancestor had a common name in a large town such as Dorchester or Bournemouth. If you are stuck and have tried other avenues, consider taking a risk and ordering a will that 'may' help you. It is never a waste of money if you find the record does not relate to you. Instead you are merely ruling out possibilities in the parish, and sometimes finding a will that does not relate to your family can be just as helpful as one that does. In this case, it is best to start with the wills that are available on Ancestry if you already have a subscription.

You are most likely to find an inventory for an ancestor if they died between 1530 and 1782 when their inventories were compulsory. These can be large documents, many pages long, and are usually very detailed as to the deceased's possessions. Each item of clothing and furniture is normally listed as well as craftsmen's tools, farm livestock and jewellery items. The estimated value is written beside each listed item giving us an idea as to the person's wealth, status and standard of living. Inventories are generally not held at the same location as the will to which it relates and it can be hard to know whether one exists for your ancestor.

Letters of administration are limited in the information that they provide, but should name the deceased's executor whom is usually their next of kin.

17. Extract from the inventory of Ann Stone of Shapwick.

Limitations of the Record

As with any historic document - and even some modern handwritten papers - the text can prove challenging to read. The older the document is, the more likely you are to have trouble deciphering the words. Most wills follow a standard format with set legal phrases; it would be a good idea to familiarise yourself with these so that they can be quickly recognised. The first few lines of a will normally give the date the will was written, the name, residence and occupation of the testator and then statements regarding the testator's physical and mental health. It is advisable to transcribe the key points from the will to save you from having to decipher it again in the future if you forget a piece of information.

Searching for an ancestor's will, particularly before 1858 as there is no central database, can be time-consuming and difficult. Readers with Dorset ancestors are lucky as a majority of their wills are on Ancestry and can easily be searched. However, just because a will is not on their website, it does not mean they did not leave one. Their will may be deposited elsewhere depending on where they lived and where they owned property at the time of their death.

There is no guarantee that any family will be named in a person's will. A person may leave their estate to their children without naming them or may choose to bequeath only to friends or colleagues. A majority of wills are of some genealogical interest; even if people are not named as the will can often give an insight into the deceased's financial status or hint at issues within the family.

As previously mentioned a married woman could not leave a will until 1883, however, you may still be able to gain an insight into her life by viewing her husband's will - if he had one. Inventories can be particularly enlightening regarding a person's belongings and in many cases it will be obvious if an object belonged to his wife rather than himself, such as items of jewellery and women's clothing.

Dorset Examples

My sixth great-grandfather, John Webb Frampton, married Elizabeth Tucker in Hampreston in 1795. Just three years later in 1798, aged twenty-four, he wrote his will. Rather unusually, he didn't change his will as he aged. This may be because he died suddenly and did not have a chance to change it, or perhaps he was simply happy with his existing will. The document was left purposefully vague, naming his wife Elizabeth as the sole executrix, but adding his estate should otherwise be left to his 'surviving child or children'. After the creation of his will, John and Elizabeth went on to have eight children, with the probate record instructing that his estate was to be split among them. This is obviously less helpful to genealogists who crave finding named children, particularly the married names of any daughters. Unusually, John named his late grandfather, Francis Pinney, a merchant of Poole, in his will. John died in Poole in 1826, with his will being proved by PCC. It is available to view on Ancestry as part of their Prerogative Court of Canterbury Wills 1384-1858 collection.

Also on Ancestry, but this time part of their Dorset Wills and Probates 1565-1858 collection, is the will of my fifth great-grandfather, Thomas Osment. Thomas is described as a miller of Sutton Poyntz with two daughters and one son, again unnamed. The will is dated 26 Jun 1794, with burial records showing Thomas was buried in nearby Preston on 1 Jul the same year. It is common to find a will being created very close to the date when a person died, and Thomas' ill health explains his very shaky signature at the bottom of the record.

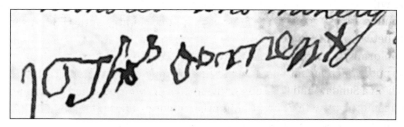

18. *Signature of Thomas Osment at the bottom of his will dated 1794.*

CHAPTER 6

Nonconformist Records

About the Record

Chances are that somewhere in your tree you will come across nonconformist ancestors - people who did not belong to the Church of England. At first this may not be obvious to you as nonconformists will often appear in parish registers. Most nonconformist chapels did not have their own burial grounds meaning they were buried at their parish church; and between 1753 and 1837 marriages were only legally recognised if they were held in the parish church, with the exception of Quakers and Jews. This meant nonconformists often opted to have a marriage ceremony in both an Anglican church and a chapel of their own faith.

There are many nonconformist denominations, the most common being Roman Catholics, Baptists, Methodists, Presbyterians, Quakers, Congregationalists and Unitarians. Some of the records you may come across mirror those of the Church of England, for example baptism, marriage and burial registers. It is important to gain an understanding of your ancestor's faith to understand the records you are looking at and how they differ from regular parish registers. For example, Baptists are baptised as adults rather than infants. It is also useful to know the name changes for each faith. The Separatists became known as Independents from the seventeenth century, and from the early nineteenth century onwards were then called Congregationalists.

It will help if you can learn a basic history of changing attitudes towards nonconformity in Britain. England was a Catholic country until 1534. A series of laws between this date and 1829 imposed a series of restrictions on nonconformists, particularly Roman Catholics. This included the 1559 Act of Uniformity which meant people were fined if they did not attend their Anglican church on a Sunday; and the 1664 Conventicles Act which banned group meetings of nonconformists with a threat of imprisonment or fines if found guilty. Catholic burial grounds were only legally allowed in England from 1853.

Whilst Roman Catholics continued to be persecuted, other denominations were granted more leniency. The 1689 Toleration Act allowed worship for non-conformists of all faiths apart from Catholicism and forced attendance at Anglican churches was lifted. It wasn't until the 1778 Catholic Relief Act that most Roman Catholic churches felt safe enough to keep their own written records, with some not starting until after the 1829 Catholic Emancipation Act.

Quakers, otherwise known as the Society of Friends, also faced a great deal of persecution until the Toleration Act of 1689. From this date, the Quakers were treated with more compassion than other faiths. They no longer had to take an oath of allegiance to the King, that other nonconformists were required to take. They were also exempt from the 1753 Marriage Act meaning they could continue to have their marriages recognised without the need to marry in an Anglican church. Quaker records differ from other nonconformist documentation too - they did not perform baptisms; marriage registers are highly detailed often naming everyone who was in attendance, and most chapels had their own burial grounds.

In 1840, the Non-Parochial Registers Act required all nonconformist baptism, marriage and burial registers to be deposited with the Registrar General. A similar reminder for the depositing of registers was made in 1857, since which registers from 1857 onwards were not handed in, although some have since been submitted to county record offices. Very few Catholic registers were surrendered.

Regardless of a person's specific nonconformist faith, there are a number of records where their names might appear, notwithstanding their own baptism and marriage registers. There were a number of nonconformist schools in the county which produced records such as attendance registers and minute books. These may also survive for some Sunday schools. People may also be found in Quarter Sessions and Assize records if they were fined for not attending their Anglican church or if they were found guilty of a non-Anglican religious meeting prior to 1689. Pipe Rolls and Recusant Rolls list nonconformists of various backgrounds including Catholics, Jews and Presbyterians. Minutes of chapel meetings are held in Dorset History Centre and these show names of those in the congregation. As with the Anglican Church, nonconformist chapels often have surviving accounts which may list pew rents, and some sects tended to have newspapers, periodicals and journals noting news within their congregations. These include the *Baptist Magazine*, the Quaker publication called the *Friend* and the *English Presbyterian Messenger*.

In 1676, Bishop Compton administered a religious survey recording the number of dissenters in each parish; this is known as the Compton census. These do not always distinguish people by faith (although Catholics are generally numbered separately) and people are generally not named. Unfortunately, Dorset holds very few of these returns compared with other counties.

An ecclesiastical census was taken in 1851 and records churches of all denominations within each district. It was a snapshot of church attendance on 31 March 1851. The records show the "sitting" or size of the congregation at each service on that day (and usually there were three services) and also notes how many "sittings" (seats) were free. It also notes the number of the Sunday scholars. Whilst no names are given, this can be a helpful document as it gives the location of what chapels existed in the parish where your ancestors lived. There were approximately 150 Methodist chapels in Dorset in 1851, compared with sixty-nine Congregationalist and Independent chapels, fifteen Baptist chapels and seven Catholic churches.

There are also a number of records which are unique to each denomination. The Wesleyan Methodist Registry 1818-1838 registered births and baptisms of children born to parents of the Wesleyan Methodist faith throughout England and Wales. Some of these date back to 1773. The Wesleyan Methodist Historic Roll dated 1898-1904 and names over one million people who contributed to the Millennium Fund. The Quakers held Yearly, Quarterly and Monthly Meetings at various levels across the country, some of the minutes of which have been published. The Surman Index is available online and lists dissenting ministers, including those who were Congregationalists, Presbyterians and Baptists.

19. *Quaker marriage record of Josiah Neave and Elizabeth Gundry.*
Dated 1812 in Shaftesbury. Both of their parents are named.

Locating the Record

Nonconformist records are spread widely across various archives and repositories. The National Archives holds many nonconformist records. The 1851 ecclesiastical census is held at HO 129. The registers that were handed into the Registrar General in 1840 and 1857 are held in RG 4-8, with some extracts available on Ancestry and Family Search websites. Later registers are either held at Dorset History Centre or may still be held by the chapel itself.

Dorset History Centre holds a large collection of nonconformist documentation. Try searching the catalogue for your ancestor's faith to see what records survive here. These include Dorford Baptist Church records from 1893, Shaftesbury and Gillingham Methodist Circuit documentation dating 1812-1997 and East Lulworth Catholic Chapel christening registers from 1815. Quarter Sessions records held at Dorset History Centre note details of fines handed to nonconformists for failing to attend their parish church. Other county record offices hold nonconformist records relating to Dorset. These include registers for the Salisbury Methodist Circuit which included some Dorset parishes, such as Sixpenny Handley, which are held by Wiltshire and Swindon History Centre and select Dorset Quaker Quarterly Meeting records held at East Sussex Record Office. These can all be searched for via one simple search on TNA's Discovery catalogue website.

The British Library holds Presbyterian journals which feature notices regarding births, marriages, deaths and obituaries amongst other articles. The Parliamentary Archives holds returns of Papists from 1705, 1767 and 1780. John Ryland's Library at the University of Manchester has a large collection of Methodist literature including journals, biographies and preaching plans detailing where preachers were working on certain dates. The collection also contains documents relating to other denominations, such as the Quakers and Baptists.

Many nonconformist records have been transcribed and published. The Catholic Record Society has published many of their registers, Recusants Rolls and Papist returns, and Somerset & Dorset Family History Society have published two volumes of the Wesleyan Methodist Historic Roll, available to purchase from their website. The original fifty volumes of this Historic Roll are held at Westminster Methodist Central Hall in London. The website www.bmdregisters.co.uk contains transcriptions of nonconformist registers that are held by The National Archives, including a large number of Quaker marriages. These records are pay-per-view on this website, or you can choose to access the information via The Genealogist, Ancestry or FindMyPast with a subscription. Check the free records on FreeREG (www.freereg.org.uk) which contain transcripts of select nonconformist register entries, as well as Anglican records.

If you have Jewish ancestry, remember that synagogues tend to hold their own historic registers. The *Jewish Chronicle* is digitised by the British Newspaper Library and features articles on bar mitzvahs and names many belonging to the faith. These can be found via a simple name search.

Where possible, visit your nonconformist ancestor's grave just as you would for an Anglican ancestor to see if the headstone provides any more detail. Jewish headstones in particular can be very detailed, whereas Quaker ones are more basic. The Memorial Inscription chapter is still relevant for nonconformist ancestors.

There are many other records unique to each faith held in a variety of locations. Through researching your ancestor's denomination you will come across other sources to research, including many freely available online. Examples include an index of Baptist Ministers' obituaries maintained by the Baptist Historical Society (www.baptisthistory.org.uk) whose website has a section devoted to family history, an index of post-1794 Unitarian obituaries (www.unitarianobituaries.org.uk) and a range of registers transcribed by OPC Dorset which vary by parish (www.

opcdorset.org). Many other records are still held by the relevant chapel. If you have found where your ancestor attended service, it is worth contacting them to find out what records they hold.

The Quaker Family History Society (https://newtrial.qfhs.co.uk) contains a great deal of information about the history of the faith as well as resources, such as wills and sufferings. The Wesley Historical Society (www.wesleyhistoricalsociety. org.uk) looks at the history of the Methodist church and features a small shop selling publications, such as *Chosen by God* by Dorothy E Graham - a list of female travelling preachers of early Methodism. Try searching online to see what other resources you can find, including if your ancestor belonged to a denomination with a smaller congregation.

Values of the Record

Knowing the characteristics of each faith can lead to genealogical discoveries. A feature of the Baptist faith was for boys to be given their mother's maiden name as a middle name. This can be seen in other denominations so it does not necessarily mean the person is a Baptist; however, when found in the registers, this is obviously very helpful when tracing the child's family tree, including his parents' marriage. It is Jewish tradition to never name your child after a living relative. Understanding this may help to narrow down a death date for a grandparent.

The Wesleyan Methodist Historic Rolls gives the names of people who donated to the cause along with their residence. In some cases a specific address is given, such as Benjamin Pearce who lived at 40 Thomas Street in Weymouth. In most cases just the town or village name is given, although this is still of interest where there are groups of people with the same surname within the same area, such as seven members of the Chinchen family residing in Witchampton. Records such as this help to discover a person's residence at a certain date and may provide leads to discover new relatives.

The values of nonconformist registers are much the same as those of the Church of England. They can be used to trace back generations within a family, including using the names of marriage witnesses to discover further family links. Many nonconformist registers are much more detailed than their Anglican counterparts, including some which name the grandparents of a child being baptised. Remember to search for your nonconformist ancestors in the Anglican registers as well, to ensure that no detail is missed.

Where preaching schedules survive, these can help you to trace a minister's movements as well as telling you what sermon was taught during that particular session. Surviving minutes of religious meetings contain names of those in the congregation, sometimes with registers of all those in attendance. It is hard to discover when a family actually converted to a new faith, but you may find records relating to their excommunication if they were punished. Some records of this survive at Dorset History Centre or within Quaker meeting minutes.

Limitations of the Record

It can be easy to be misled by nonconformist chapel records. Whereas a majority of towns and villages had their own Anglican churches, nonconformist chapels were more widespread; not every parish would have a Methodist chapel for example. This means that whereas we can usually use the parish registers to find where our ancestors were residing, we cannot do so with nonconformist registers with the same confidence. If your ancestor was a Baptist, then they may have had to travel a fair way to attend their nearest Baptist chapel. Many Catholics even travelled abroad in order to have their marriage legally recognised within their own faith. Therefore never assume that the chapel records your nonconformist ancestor is found in, is in the same parish as the one they reside.

People often changed their religion and this makes it more difficult to trace them. It can be hard to keep track of what faith your ancestors were following and to know which records to search next. Your ancestor may have been baptised into the Anglican church, married in a Methodist ceremony, be seen attending a Baptist church and then be buried at an Anglican church. Knowing where to find an ancestor who is missing from the parish registers can be tricky. Pay attention to any clues of nonconformity, such as 'Papist' written in parish register column for Roman Catholics, missing appearances in baptism registers and naming of children from Old Testament names, which may hint towards a Protestant faith.

20. *Extract from the Catholic register of St. Mary's Chapel at Lulworth Castle, 1834. The register is written in Latin.*

Nonconformist documents can sometimes be harder to interpret than Anglican records. Catholic registers are usually written in Latin. Some entries in nonconformist registers were made retrospectively, sometimes many years after the event. This was particularly common with baptisms. If the dates in the register appear to be out of order then this may explain why. If it looks as though your ancestor's event was recorded after the date itself, be wary that this makes it less reliable and the date may be incorrect. There are also many examples of a family baptising their children all together on the same date and it is not always possible to tell how old the children were at this time or who the eldest and youngest children were.

There is a higher rate of loss amongst nonconformist registers compared with Anglican registers. Not only were some destroyed, many were never created in the first place. The survival rate varies between faiths with Quakers known for their excellent record keeping whereas Methodists were more lax. Methodists often did not record marriages or burials which can lead to frustration for family historians who may never find the date of a relevant family event or proof of parentage.

Dorset Examples

My husband's fifth great-grandparents, Jane Florence and Philip Osmond, were Wesleyan Methodists residing for most of their life in Lytchett Matravers. They married in Spetisbury in 1808 in the parish church, due to the necessity at the time to marry in a Church of England ceremony. Their children were all baptised in the Wesleyan chapel in Poole, the register of which survives at The National Archives and is available to see on Ancestry in their collection of nonconformist and non-parochial registers. The details given include the child's name, their parents' names, their sex, parish where they were born, child's date of birth, date of the baptism and who performed the ceremony. For example, their eldest son George was born 11 Sep 1809 and baptised 17 Oct 1809 by John Simmons. His parents are named and his birthplace of Lytchett Matravers is stated.

When researching Jane's ancestry it became a little unclear and there were a few different options as to who her parents may be. Interestingly, her parentage was confirmed by her daughter Elizabeth's baptism record. Elizabeth was born in 1820 when the appearance of the baptism register had been changed with spaces for more information. The new format required a record of the name of the mother's parents, in this case George and Elizabeth Florence, which in turn helped me to confirm Jane's baptism in Spetisbury in 1786. The transcription of this record does not currently give this parentage information on Ancestry, hence the importance of always viewing the image of the original record.

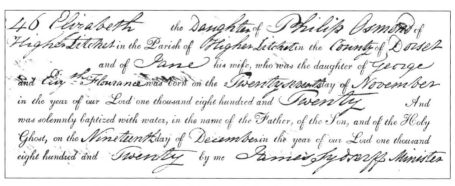

21. *The baptism of Elizabeth Osmond of Lytchett Matravers, 1820.*
Note the mother's parents are also named.

CHAPTER 7
Business and Work Records

About the Records

Many people discover their ancestor's occupation but then fail to research this any further. You might find out from a census that your ancestor was a publican or find out from a burial register that the deceased worked as a blacksmith. Whilst it is interesting to know what their occupation was, by researching this further you can gain a real insight into their lives. After all, we spend a great deal of our lives at work and it was the same for our ancestors. Not only can we learn what their day-to-day lives would have been like, occupational records can also provide us with other useful genealogical information and can lead us to new discoveries.

This chapter will look at occupational records but regrettably it cannot cover them all. There is a huge range of jobs that have a variety of records associated with them, and some occupations have left more records than others. Whatever occupation your ancestor had, I recommend that you research this as much as you can. Look into what daily activities the role involved at the time your ancestor was known to be working; and investigate the pay, working conditions and hours they would likely have been working. Even if a specific occupational record naming your ancestor fails to exist, you can still gain a general understanding of their working life. Some of the more common jobs in Dorset are looked at further in the 'Dorset Occupations' chapter.

From 1563, all apprentices entering a trade required a written contract between them and the master who was to teach them their craft. Apprenticeships normally lasted for seven years, with the apprentice being aged between ten and eighteen at the beginning of their training. You will most commonly find a person as an apprentice between the ages of fourteen and twenty-one. The master was often a relative, such as the apprentice's father or uncle; so often just knowing the names of the parties involved can give you a new lead. The indentures serve as proof of the apprentice's change in their parish of legal settlement and can explain why people moved between parishes.

If your ancestor was in the clergy there are many fantastic resources out there for you to inspect. Your first port of call should be theclergydatabase.org.uk which gives you a great starting point for your research. A simple name search can provide a lot of biographical information which is cited with its sources. These sources may include the Clergy List (from 1841), the Clerical Guide (1817) and the Clerical Directory (from 1858). Ordination papers may include a baptism certificate and

48

testimonials from fellows. These sources can help you to form a well-rounded picture of a person's clerical career. To get an idea of your clergy ancestor's daily working life, look at the vestry minutes and parish registers to see what they were up to week by week and what events they were involved in within their parish of incumbency.

Those of you with ancestors working in the legal profession also have a good range of occupational records to explore. Publications include the Law List (from 1775) and Men at the Bar (Foster 1885), as well as alumni records and certificates of admission to court. If your ancestor worked as a barrister, they would most likely have gone to Oxford or Cambridge University before continuing their training at the Inns of Court in London. If your ancestor was a solicitor, however, university was not necessary and a majority of them were apprenticed instead.

If you are researching someone who worked in the medical profession, you may find them in the Army List or Navy List if they worked in the forces. They may also feature in the Medical Directory (1845), the Roll of the College of Physicians or in the records of the Society of Apothecaries.

> Otthen, Edward; demy MAGDALEN COLL. 1596-1606 B.A. 10 July 1600, M.A. 27 March 1604; vicar of Whitchurch Canonicorum, Dorset, 1609; Died 26 Sept, 1617

22. Edward Otthen's entry from Alumni Oxonienses.

If your ancestor had their own trade, you may find them in a trade directory or advertising in a local newspaper. People had to pay to appear in trade directories but despite this, they were often used by tradesmen as they were a key source of advertising. Examples include *Pigot & Co, Post Office, Hunt & Co, J G Harrod & Co, Mercer & Crocker's* and *Kelly's Directories*. They are generally organised with an alphabetical surname listing under each parish. For example, the 1855 Post Office Directory for Cheselbourne lists sixteen people alphabetically by surname from Reverend Thomas Wickham Birch to George Tett, a farmer and miller. Others are arranged by parish and then by occupation, such as the 1851 Hunt & Co Directory for Shaftesbury which lists a large number of people under headings such as bakers, shoemakers, cheese dealers, hairdressers and auctioneers.

More than a quarter of a million people were employed by the railway network in the late nineteenth century. On my mother's side of the family are direct ancestors who worked as a stationmaster, train driver, signalman, fireman (stoker) and a railway carpenter. Unfortunately Dorset lost much of its railway network as a result of the Beeching Report in 1963. Many stations were closed in the years that followed including Blandford and Wimborne.

It can of course be helpful to see where our ancestors once worked. This could involve discovering a photograph of their work place such as an inn, public house, ship or factory. These may be found at Dorset History Centre, online or in local history books. Alternatively, where no photographs survive, viewing images and maps of the area where they worked can help you to place their occupation on the landscape. Try plotting their daily route to work and see how long this would have taken them each day.

23. *Wm Taylor Ltd 'The Cycle Man' in Parkstone.*

Locating the Record

Many published occupational sources are available free online with Google Books. These include the *Clerical Guide* and *Fasti Ecclesiae Anglicanae*, the latter of which names those who ranked archdeacon or above. If your ancestor required university education for their occupation, the alumni records are also available online or via Ancestry. Search for Alumni Oxonienses, Alumni Cantabrigienses or Alumni Dublinenses, depending on whether they studied at Oxford, Cambridge or Dublin. The records of the Society of Apothecaries are held at the Guildhall Library, with a name index at the Society of Genealogists. The Guildhall Library and Society of Genealogists also hold the Roll of the College of Physicians, with some entries available on FindMyPast. Many trade directories can be viewed online at Ancestry, The Internet Archive (https://archive.org) or Guildhall Library. Many are also free to view online at http://specialcollections.le.ac.uk/. Some transcriptions are available on www.opcdorset.org for select Dorset parishes.

Dorset History Centre holds a good selection of apprenticeship indentures and company records. These include the records of Stewart's Garden Centre in Ferndown 1850 -1999, Poole Pottery 1855-2010 and Cosens and Company 1859 - 1997. It is worth searching the catalogue when you have discovered a company that your ancestor worked at, to see if any records are held at the archives. Dorset History Centre have an index of Dorset photographers 1840 -1900, a list of twentieth-century Dorset thatchers and many articles relating to brewing in the county. It also holds recognizance registers naming innkeepers who pledged to keep their house in good order. There is an early example for Lyme Regis 1598 -1612 and a later listing from Dorchester 1795 -1828. You may be able to trace generations of the same family running an inn by tracing back through those records. Be imaginative when looking for occupational records relating to your ancestor when you're at the county record office. Your ancestor may be named in churchwarden accounts within parish records if they were paid for a service, such as carpentry or masonry.

The National Archives holds a large collection of occupational records. These include records of railway workers, including Somerset and Dorset Railway records for 1863 -1877 in series RAIL 627/6 and Somerset and Dorset Joint Line Committee for 1877-1928 in RAIL 626/44-53 and RAIL 972/1. TNA also holds records relating to those in the coastguard service, people working as civil or Crown servants and has a good collection of records relating to artists, especially those that were employed by the government. In CP 37 at TNA are the Rolls of Oaths of Allegiance dating 1784 -1836 within which you should find any clergymen ancestors.

Online genealogy sites are rapidly increasing their occupation record holdings. Ancestry has Dorset Alehouse Licence Records 1754 -1821, railway employment records 1833 -1956, postal service appointment books 1737-1969, nursing registers 1891-1968 and medical professional registers 1615 -1980. FindMyPast has the 1925 Dental Surgeons' Directory, teachers' registration council registers 1914 -1948 and the Dorset Hemp and Flax Growers list 1782-1793. This latter record is also available to purchase from Somerset and Dorset Family History Society. The Genealogist has *Biographia Dramatica* which lists actors 1500s -1811, bankruptcy lists 1786 -1806 and the roll of army medical staff 1727-1898.

Register Entry concerning :	**HANDLEY, HENRIETTA MARIA.**		
Date of Registration :	**1st November, 1914.**	Register Number :	**4210.**
~~Professional~~ Address :	**White Heather, Clarendon Road,**		
	BROADSTONE, Dorset.		

24. *Extract from Henrietta Maria Handley's entry in the Teachers' Registration Council Register, 1914.*

Also online you will find the registers of the money received for the payment on taxes for an apprentice's indenture, known as Stamp Duty, 1710 -1811. These registers record the money masters paid for a trade in order to have an apprentice and were kept by the Commissioners of Stamps. These can be viewed at Ancestry.

If your ancestor worked for the East India Company, annual employee lists survive from 1803 at the British Library, together with other related records such as registers of births, marriages and burials of its employees in India.

Some occupations required a licence to practise, such as gamekeepers, midwives and publicans. These may be found at Dorset History Centre or TNA. Licences were required to run an inn from 1617. The regulations for this were relaxed from 1830 which led to an increase in public houses. These licence applications and renewals can be found in local newspapers. Newspapers are a great source for researching a business. Articles include notices about liquidation and bankruptcy, as well as advertisements; these are most interesting if your ancestor was self-employed. Other articles may record notable accidents in the workplace or milestones that the company reached. You may also find criminal charges in newspapers, such as theft from the workplace or a landlord failing to keep an 'orderly house'.

BLANDFORD.

TRANSFER OF LICENCE.—The licence of the Greyhound Inn, lately in the occupation of Mrs. Rolls, has been transferred to Mr. R. Eyers, of the Crown Hotel.

25. Newspaper article detailing the licence transfer of the Greyhound Inn in Blandford Forum from Mrs Rolls to Mr Eyers, 1865.

Remember to check out any museums too relating to your ancestor's occupation. They may not have a document or object that directly relates to your ancestor, but they can certainly help you to understand more about what their job entailed. Examples in Dorset include the Grove Prison Museum on Portland which would interest descendants of prison workers and the Water Supply Museum in Sutton Poyntz which is of interest if your ancestors helped extend the water supply to the area. Many other occupational museums exist throughout the country that may be worth a visit. Some of them go above and beyond to help you understand what your ancestor's life may have been like. For example, Chiltern Open Air Museum offers a Blacksmith Experience Day where you can spend four hours working in a Victorian forge. Don't forget to also visit the museum local to your ancestor's place of residence. Most general museums, such as Poole Museum, Blandford Town Museum and Sherborne Museum have exhibits relating to local occupations. Other museums across the country may also hold records, such as the National Maritime Museum, which holds records of shipping companies.

Finally, if your ancestor worked for a company that still exists, try contacting them for information. Many companies have large archives holding documents of interest such as staff magazines featuring personal announcements, wage books and staff records. Other businesses have handed in their records to county record offices so it is worth checking Dorset History Centre's catalogue for any relevant holdings. A majority of historical business documentation has unfortunately been destroyed.

Values of the Record

Apprenticeship indentures serve as proof of the apprentice's change in their parish of legal settlement and can explain why people moved between parishes. They may also give you a new lead in your research if the named master is a relative of the apprentice. At the very least, whether you are researching the apprentice or the master, you can know what trade they worked in, when and where this took place.

Some occupations leave a good paper trail which is fairly easy to access and research, such as lawyers, clergy and surgeons. The records of some roles, such as those in the police and railways, are being digitised at an increasing rate. The amount of information we can gain from these records varies but they all help you learn more about a person's role. They may reveal your ancestor's wage, their length of service in a company, reasons for dismissal, injuries occurred at work or give personal information such as their date of birth and residence.

Ancestors who studied at university and worked in a specialised area are more likely to have moved far from their parish of birth. If your ancestor was born in Dorset and studied at Oxford or Cambridge, they may not have returned to the county. Likewise, you may find that an ancestor was born elsewhere in the country but chose to settle in Dorset. Fortunately, the alumni records usually give enough detail to help trace where a person came from, what they studied and where they spent their career.

Trade directories can be used to trace an ancestor's movements, depending on where his business was based. You may find the handing over of management from a father to a son if it was a family-run business. Directories also feature advertisements and a brief history of the region, often with geographical details which can be of interest if you are unfamiliar with the parish.

Freemason registers and freedom rolls of guilds can help you to learn more about your ancestor's occupation, residence, age and provide you with the knowledge that they belonged to a specific group. For example, the Freemason registers, as seen on Ancestry, list Jonathan Bridell of Maiden Newton, a forty-four-year-old haberdasher who was admitted as a member on the 25 Jun 1781.

When you have searched all avenues for records relating to your ancestor's work, put them into chronological order to make sense of them; creating this visual timeline will perhaps explain that they moved parish due to the husband's work changing. This is particularly helpful with occupations such as publicans who often moved between public houses, taking their families with them to a new parish. Depending on what information you find, the records may also show their changing salary or declining health forcing them to take less physical roles. Indeed, knowing an ancestor's occupation can help you to understand why they were afflicted with certain ailments; those working with felt, such as hatters, often developed dementia due to working with mercury, which led to the phrase *mad as a hatter*.

If your ancestor changed their occupation suddenly, then it is worth exploring the possible reasons for this. It may not be possible to draw a firm conclusion as to why, but your research may help you gain an understanding as to why this may have happened. You may discover that their company closed forcing the employees to find new work, or perhaps they were dismissed from their job due to a criminal charge. By locating as many occupational records as you can and researching their line of work, you will give yourself the best opportunity to understand the challenges your ancestor faced in their lifetime.

Limitations of the Record

As with pauper apprenticeships arranged by the parish, regular apprenticeships also often failed to be completed. This may be due to the death or illness of the master or perhaps because the apprentice failed to meet the occupational standards or just decided to escape ill-treatment. Therefore, just because you find your ancestor was an apprentice tailor does not mean that they completed the full term or ever went on to work was a tailor themselves.

Trade directories are usually around one year out of date by the time of their publication, so don't be misled by an ancestor appearing in the directory and whom you thought died eight months before he's listed! Directories can still often be used as a rough guide to look for a person's death or relocation to another parish, but bear in mind this retrospective publication date.

Many of the occupational records left behind are rather limited as to the information they can provide. There are many registers with employees' named but no other identifiable information, such as their age or residence. This can make it hard to prove that a named person is the correct person that we are researching. There is a big difference between records left behind by different occupations. You may find an ancestor who worked as a publican left a long trail of documentation whereas an ancestor who worked as a shopkeeper left seemingly nothing; and remember many occupational records have been destroyed.

Foot Jane (Mrs.), farmer
Frampton Robert George, *Red Lion*
Holloway Thomas, dairyman
Legg Ahuzzath, farmer
Martin William, farmer, Moor court
Meatyard William, *Churchill Arms*
Mullett Henry, farmer
Patten Gideon, grocer, draper, general outfitters & ironmonger

26. Extract from Kelly's Directory of 1880 for Sturminster Marshall.

Where no records have survived for a certain ancestor's occupation, it is helpful to gain a general idea about what their work would have involved. Make sure you acknowledge that this is just a rough guide and your ancestor may have had their own way of working or worked irregular hours. We are also unlikely to be able to discover what a person thought of their job, whether they enjoyed it, whether they ever considered changing roles or any charity work they did. It was common to find sons following in their father's footsteps and you may find generations of males working in the same occupation. However, sometimes it is not possible to know why a son chose a certain occupation that was different from his father's job.

Dorset Examples
The amount of information you will find out about your ancestor's occupations will vary. My sixth great-grandfather, John Webb Frampton, was born in Poole in 1774. In 1792, he appears in FindMyPast Country Apprentices records as an apprentice mercer to master John Rogers in Newport on the Isle of Wight. The next mention of his occupation is when he wrote his will in 1798 in which he is described as an innkeeper in Longham. By 1800 he is recorded as being a shopkeeper in Poole when he was found guilty for using faulty weights in order to overcharge his customers - not his finest hour! In 1816, in a recognizance, John is noted as being a gentleman. A recognizance is a bond that a person undertakes before a court or magistrate, agreeing to carry out a certain act. This was usually agreeing to return to court at a later date. The latter two documents are both held at Dorset History Centre.

Other ancestors of mine have considerably less information about their occupations. My sixth great-grandfather, Thomas Paul, is listed as a thatcher in the 1758 militia records in Fordington. In 1780, Thomas is listed as a master thatcher, training his apprentice son John in the trade. This indenture is held at Southampton Archives. Likewise, my seventh great-grandfather, Stephen Squibb of Sutton Poyntz, is noted in the country apprentices' records as being a master to his apprentice son Robert, teaching him the trade of being a velmonger - this was someone who dealt

27. Register of Duties showing Stephen Squibb as master to his son Robert,
Their relationship is not stated in the record.

with the stomachs of calves fed entirely on milk, which were used for making rennet which is required to produce cheese.

As a different example, John Pett began working as a grocer and tea dealer in Dorchester before taking on the duty of postmaster for the town. His occupation as a grocer was first mentioned in the Freeman Admission Records when he was admitted as a Freemason at the Durnovarian Lodge in Dorchester in 1814. Grocers typically sold dried goods such as sugar, spices, rice and coffee, whilst greengrocers sold fruit and vegetables which was a different trade. John can be seen in various records trading as a grocer between the first evidence of his occupation in 1814 and his last entry in Pigot's Directory of 1830, showing he was successful despite local competition in the trade. John Pett can also be seen in Land Tax Returns between 1815 and 1819; he is listed as the occupier of a building belonging to George Frampton. Sources show the business where John worked was previously known as *Frampton's Grocery Shop,* situated in High East Street.

The British Postal Service Appointment book of 1818 shows John was appointed as postmaster on 16 Dec 1818, taking over from George Frampton who had resigned. John is listed here as a grocer and tea dealer. Purpose-built Post Offices did not appear in England until 1850 so prior to this, local tradesmen such as John ran the local postal service. For John, working as a postmaster would have meant reliable work and income. In the 1830 Pigot's Directory there are six grocers listed in Dorchester. By the time of Robson's Directory in 1839, there are fifteen. This implies there was more competition in the area, especially as six of these grocers were situated at High East Street when John was based.

John remained postmaster of Dorchester until 1845, serving for twenty-six

Mr. Francis Lock, of Blandford, has been appointed Post-master of Dorchester, on the resignation of Mr. Pett, who, for the long period of 26 years (having been appointed in January, 1819,) has discharged the arduous and responsible duties of his office with unremitting care and attention, and to the general satisfaction of the inhabitants. Few men ever retired from a local public office more respected than Mr. Pett.

28. Article naming Francis Lock as John Pett's successor as Postmaster of Dorchester.

56

years. An article about his retirement featured in the *Sherborne Mercury* on 3 Jan 1846 where it is stated that John *has resigned from his arduous and responsible duties*. John was clearly highly regarded in his community, with the article noting that *few men ever retired from a local public office more respected than Mr Pett*. It is noted in the *Sherborne Mercury* on 19 Dec 1846 that John was absent from the annual tradesmen's dinner due to ill health. It is the last time John features in an historical record before his death. Sadly, John only had a short retirement, passing away on 11 Aug 1849.

CHAPTER 8

Military Sources

About the Record

Some people have a family steeped in military history and will become familiar with the methods needed when researching soldiers from various time periods in different services. Most of us will have someone in our tree who has served in the military at some point. If your ancestors didn't fight in either of the World Wars, you may come across them in the records before 1913. If your ancestor was an officer then their records are generally stored separately from those of other ranks. Don't assume that because your ancestor was from Dorset that they served with the Dorset Regiment. Whilst this was true for my paternal grandfather, my husband's grandfather, Vernon O'Shea who was born and lived in Dorset, served with the Gordon Highlanders, based in Scotland. No matter what regiment they served in or what county they lived in, the records are largely held at The National Archives (TNA). The best place to start is with any military paraphernalia that your ancestor left behind that may give details as to their regiment or service number. The records in this chapter are grouped so you can easily refer to whichever service is relevant to your ancestor. Note that not every record will be available for a person in service, with many records being lost.

Locating the Records – Army Pre-WWI

For those attempting to search for their ancestor's military records for the first time, the process can appear confusing. There is no single database and searching online on various military history websites is tricky and often has mixed results. Below is a list detailing the document type, where it is found at TNA, the year it relates to, whether they relate to soldiers (S) or officers (O) and the details the record usually contains.

Soldiers' Service Records 1760-1913 - WO 97(S)

- Age and place of birth
- Previous occupation
- Date and place of enlistment
- Summary of military career
- Discharge date
- Affidavits

Description Books 1795-1900 - WO 25 (S)
- Age and place of birth
- Occupation
- Military service

Casualty Lists 1797-1910 - WO 25 (S)
- Birth place
- Next of kin
- Rank
- Personal effects
- Occupation

Pension Lists 1715-1857 - WO 25 (S/O)
- Name
- Pension rate
- Date pension awarded

Muster Books and Pay Lists 1732-1999 - WO 12 (WO 69 for Artillery) (S/O)
- Enlistment and discharge dates
- Soldiers' and officers' locations
- Rank
- Pay

Campaign Medals 1793-1949 - WO 100 (S/O)
- Name
- Medal awarded

Army Lists 1702-Present - WO 64-66 and WO 211 (O)
- Name
- Regiment details

Widows' Pensions 1713-1921 - WO 23-25 and PMG 9-11 (O)
- Name
- Pension rate

Officers' Service Records 1764-1913 - WO 25 and WO 76 (O)
- Name
- Age
- Rank
- Marriage details
- Children

Half-pay Records 1713-1921 - WO 23-25 (O)

- Name
- Rank
- Regiment
- Location upon payment
- Some provide date of death

Locating the Records – Army WWI and WWII

Officers' records from WWI were largely destroyed in WWII. Reconstructed officers' records are held at TNA at WO339 and WO374. Many soldiers' records were also destroyed, explaining why so many people have trouble finding the relevant records for their ancestor - many no longer exist! Below is a list following the same format as that above relating this time to WWI soldiers.

Records of Service - WO 363 and WO 364
(Service Papers for the Household Cavalry are at WO 400)

- Name
- Age
- Date of enlistment
- Next of kin
- Address
- Service summary
- Medical information
- Discharge date

Medal Rolls - WO 100-102 and WO 390

- Name
- Regiment
- Medal awarded

War Diaries - WO 95 and The Keep Military Museum

- Regiment activities (few people are named)

Casualty Lists - Published on Ancestry and FindMyPast
Under 'Soldiers Died in the Great War' and 'Officers Died in the Great War'

- Name
- Place of birth (sometimes)
- Enlistment

Commonwealth War Grave Commission (CWGC) - www.cwgc.org
- Name
- Age
- Next of kin
- Regiment
- Date and place of death
- Service number
- Place of burial

WWI Dorset Casualties - https://dorsetinthegreatwar.co.uk/
- Listing of those named on War Memorials across Dorset
- Also includes those from Dorset listed on memorials outside of the county

The Keep Military Museum holds a variety of potentially useful material relating to Dorset (and Devon) regiments. Their collection includes a selection of war diaries, the 1918 list of Dorset Absent Voters and photographs of largely unnamed soldiers. You can pay for researchers at the museum to look through their collection for any relevant mention of your ancestor.

There is only limited information available regarding those in all the Armed Forces who served after WWI. The records are held by the Ministry of Defence and can be accessed via their online application service. There is usually quite a long wait to receive the records. The records will vary according to when they fought but information usually includes age, date and place of enlistment, summary of service (usually just locations and dates) and next of kin. These WWII service records are currently being moved to The National Archives with an estimated completion date of 2028. The process to apply for these records should then be simplified. The CWGC also covers WWII. Records regarding those who were Prisoners of War during this period are available on Ancestry and FindMyPast. A certain amount of information can be gathered from reading printed regimental histories and by visiting regimental museums.

Locating the Records – Royal Navy Officers

Royal Navy officers and ratings (lower ranks) are researched very differently. Publications such as Charnock's *Biographia Navalis*, Marshall's *Royal Navy Biography* and O'Byrne's *A Naval Biographical Dictionary* are the easiest places to begin searching for a Royal Navy officer. They list officers by name with details about their career such as promotions through the ranks.

Below describes the further sources used to search for a Royal Navy officer. The following list regarding Royal Navy ratings also features records that name officers.

Passing Certificates 1691-1902 - ADM 6, ADM 13 and ADM 106-7
- Name
- Age
- Place of birth
- Service summary

Half-pay Registers 1693-1924 – ADM 25 and PMG 15
- Name
- Pay rate
- Address (sometimes)

Black Books 1741-1815 - ADM 11-12
- Names of Officers who were guilty of misconduct who were not to be re-employed

Service Records 1756-1931 – ADM 196 (some on FindMyPast)
- Name
- Date and place of birth
- Address
- Marriage details

Navy List 1782-Present – Online (Ancestry, FindMyPast etc)
- Name
- Rank
- Ship
- Location (details vary)

Surveys 1817-1861 – ADM 9
- Name
- Rank
- Promotion date
- Summary of military career

War Graves Roll and Naval Casualties 1914-1933 - ADM 242
- Name
- Date of death

Locating the Records – Royal Navy Ratings
- Ratings will regrettably not appear in the above sources. See the list below for the best sources to trace a rating's career.

Ships' Musters and Pay Books 1667-1878 – ADM 36-39, ADM 41 and others (Check at TNA) (O/R)
- Name
- Ship's name
- Date of hospitalisation or death
- Age and place of birth (from 1764)

Medal Rolls 1793-1995 - ADM 171 (O/R)
- Name and medal or clasp awarded

Certificates of Service 1802-1894 - ADM 29 (O/R)
- Name and record of military service

Battle of Trafalgar Database 1805 – www.nationalarchives.gov.uk/trafalgarancestors (O/R)
- Name
- Age
- Birth place
- Rank
- Service summary (details vary)

WWI Lives at Sea Database 1914-1918 - https://royalnavyrecordsww1.rmg.co.uk (O/R)
- Name
- Service number
- Previous occupation
- Date and place of birth
- Discharge date
- Service summary
- General details of ships movements and action seen

Pension Records 1737-1854 - ADM 6 (R)
- Name
- Date of death
- Disability
- Ship's name

Allotment Registers 1795-1852 - ADM 27 (R)
- Name
- Next of kin
- Wage details
- Note: No records for 1812-1829

Continuous Service Engagement Books 1853-1872 - ADM 139 (R)
- Name
- Date and place of birth
- Physical description
- Summary of service

Register of Seamen's Services 1873-1924 - ADM 188 (R)
- Name
- Date and place of birth
- Physical description
- Summary of service

Commonwealth War Graves Commission 1914-1947 – www.cwgc.org (O/R)
- Name
- Age
- Next of kin
- Date and place of death
- Service number
- Place of burial

If your ancestor served in the Royal Navy, they may have gone on to work in the Coastguard. Many records relating to this service is held at ADM175 including discharge records for 1858 -1868 and Admiralty appointments for 1819 -1866. PMG23 holds pension records for 1857-1935.

Locating the Records – Other Forces
Not all of our military ancestors were in the army or navy. Below are lists detailing records applicable to the other services.

Royal Air Force

Service Records 1914-1919 – WO 363-264
- Name, age, enlistment date
- Next of kin and address
- Service summary
- Medical information
- Discharge date

Casualty Lists 1914-1919 – Published (Ancestry and FindMyPast)
Under 'Soldiers Died in the Great War' and 'Officers Died in the Great War'
- Name
- Place of birth (sometimes)
- Enlistment

Commonwealth War Graves Commission 1914-1947 – www.cwgc.org
- Name
- Age
- Next of kin
- Date and place of death
- Service number
- Place of burial

Air Force List 1914-1919 – AIR 76 (Officers only)
Entries were made retrospectively from 1918
- Name
- Date of birth
- Next of kin
- Address
- Units
- Medals awarded

Royal Marines

Army List 1702-Present – WO 64-66 and WO 211 (Officers only)
- Name
- Regiment details

Navy List 1797-Present – Online at Ancestry and FindMyPast (Officers only)
- Name
- Rank
- Location (details vary)

Attestation Forms 1790-1925 – ADM 157
- Name and place of birth
- Occupation and physical description
- Summary of service

Description Books 1755-1940 – ADM 158
- Name
- Age
- Place of birth
- Date and place of enlistment

Royal Marines' Wills 1786-1909 – ADM 48
- Search wills by name for all ranks

Medal Rolls 1793-1972 – ADM 171
- Name
- Division
- Medals and clasps issued

Service Records 1842-1925 – ADM 196 (Officers only) and ADM 159 (Other ranks)
- Name
- Date and place of birth
- Occupation
- Religion
- Physical description
- Summary of service

Merchant Navy

Musters 1747-1860 – BT 98
- Master's name
- Port
- Ship
- Sometimes crew members are named

Crew Lists 1835-1860 – BT 98
- Crew name
- Port

Crew Lists 1860-1938 – BT 99
- Crew name
- Port
- Only a 10% sample has been retained

Dorset Crew Lists 1863-1914 – Ancestry
- Crew name
- Port
- Name of ship's owner
- Master's name and residence

Register of Seamen's Tickets 1845-1854 – BT 113 and FindMyPast
- Name
- Date and place of birth
- Address
- Summary of service

Register of Masters 1845-1854 – BT 115
- Name, date and place of birth
- Address
- Summary of service

Masters' and Mates' Certificates 1850-1927 – National Maritime Museum and Ancestry
- Name, date and place of birth
- Issue port and date
- Address
- Service history

Register of Seamen 1853-1856 – BT 116 and FindMyPast
- Name
- Place of birth
- Age
- Service details

Central Index Register of Merchant Seamen 1918-1941 – Southampton Archives and FindMyPast
- Name
- lace and year of birth
- Rank
- Service details

Register of Merchant Seamen's Services 1941-1972– BT 382
- Name
- Date and place of birth
- Rank
- Summary of service

Medal Rolls (WWII) 1939-1945 – BT 395
- Name
- Date and place of birth
- Medals awarded

The Merchant Navy crew lists available on Ancestry for 1863-1938 are particularly useful. For example, in 1903 the SS *Rifleman* is shown to have been owned by Albert Lane of Lyme Regis with John Gardner of the same town acting as its Master. Many of these records, including this one, are not yet indexed by name so will need to be browsed by port to find your ancestor. Boat movements can often be tracked via newspaper records. For example, on 2 Aug 1888 the *Shields Daily Gazette* notes that the *Rifleman* of Lyme Regis sailed from Hull the previous Tuesday.

Locating the Records – Musters and Militia Records

You may find that none of your ancestors served with any of the above. Many people assume that everyone's grandparents and great-grandparents served in the World Wars but this certainly wasn't always the case. A large number of men did not take part in the wars, sometimes because they chose not to on moral grounds; they were possibly medically unfit or might have been needed elsewhere for crucial work towards the war effort. Your ancestors further back are more likely to feature in military records, particularly where lists of men who would be able to fight were taken in parishes - even if they never served. The militia was a reserve force of non-professional soldiers.

Below is a list of some of the potential records you may use for this purpose and where those for Dorset are held.

Tudor and Stuart Musters 1522-1649 – TNA and Dorset History Centre
- Names of men aged 15-60 (the poor were excluded)
- Any weaponry the men owned

Militia Lists 1757-1831 – TNA, Dorset History Centre and Ancestry
- Names of men aged 18-45 (up to 50 until 1762)
- Occupation
- Disability
- Tithing of residence

Posse Comitatus 1798 –Dorset History Centre and Ancestry
- Names of men aged 15-60
- Occupation
- Height
- Some relationships are stated

Levée en Masse 1803/4 –Dorset History Centre and Ancestry
- Names of men aged 15-55
- Occupation
- Disability

Values of the Record

The obvious value of all of the above records is the amount of detail they reveal. This means not only can they tell us about the military service of our ancestor, but also help us to gain useful information such as their birth date, birth place and next of kin. Do ensure that you carefully read any military record you view to gain as much information as possible from it. Records from WWI and WWII often contain codes and military abbreviations which mean nothing to most of us, but a quick look on a search-engine will tell you what they mean. For example, codes on WWI military records can tell you if your ancestor was discharged on medical grounds, if he was unlikely to become an effective soldier or if they died during service.

29. Excerpt from the attestation form of 18-year-old Henry Hatcher of Bincombe who enlisted into the Dorset Regiment in 1914.

Older musters and militia records are great for tracking the location of the adult male members of a family and are often used as a census substitute. If you are having trouble locating a family in the parish registers, you may find the adult male in a muster or militia record located in a certain tithing. This was an administrative unit equivalent to one tenth of a hundred or wapentake. Identification can sometimes prove tricky, but they can certainly give you a hint as to which parish registers to search. Dorset was the first county in Britain to raise its own militia and has the earliest militia records, dating from 6 Aug 1757. In certain cases the militia records for Dorset are particularly detailed - for example, ages are given in the 1759 list for Langton Matravers.

The *Posse Comitatus* and *Levée en Masse* are lists of reservists who could be called upon if the French invaded England. The *Posse Comitatus* can be of particular interest. This notes if a man was married and how many children he had- usually just those aged ten and under. Some Dorset examples list father's names, brother's names and if they were unmarried. Other military records tend to name the next of kin, generally a spouse or parent, and sometimes name their children.

If you have found the name of the ship upon which your ancestor served, try to see if there are any paintings, models or photographs of it. If the ship was wrecked,

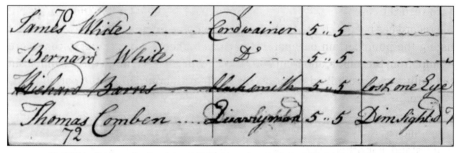

30. *Militia List from Portland dated 1796. Note that the infirmities for Richard Barns and Thomas Comben are stated as 'lost one eye' and 'dim sighted' respectively.*

a modern photograph of the wreckage may be found. Try searching www.wrecksite.eu to discover the details of the current location of the wreck and any further details, such as number of deaths which occurred as a result of the wreckage.

Certain military records note what a man's occupation was before enlisting and this can help to trace his earlier occupational records, including staff registers and apprenticeship records. It may also help to identify him from other records, such as the census. A man may have returned to the same trade after his military career ended, but not always, so keep an open mind when tracing later records.

A man's military service is often a huge part of his life. When I wrote my maternal grandfather's autobiography, his service with the Royal Signals in World War II took up a large part of the text. Funnily enough he never spoke to me about his time during the war, but I was able to piece together his service history from some notes he left behind and other paraphernalia. So take time to properly search a person's military career. For many men, their time in service changed them forever, gave them new strengths, a different outlook and a better appreciation of life. Unfortunately of course, not all men came home safely and so researching your ancestor's military career may help you to understand the last few months or years of their life.

Limitations of the Record

Military records of course will only contain details of those who served in the military and those of their family. Until recent times this means the records only focus on men. Those unfit to fight will also be much less likely to be listed. Sometimes men enlisted only to be discharged due to ill health at a later date and some militia records record all adult men but note if a person is infirm; sometimes the detail of the disability is noted which can be of interest.

It can sometimes be frustrating if your ancestor does not appear in any military records, especially if they were of a 'fighting age' at the time - whether that is in the 1798 Posse Comitatus or in WWI records. It can help to research the limitations of each record to discover why they may not appear. It could be that they fought but the record has been lost. Other reasons for their absence include early musters not listing the poor, certain occupations such as teachers and the clergy that were exempt from the militia, and from 1802 a man with young children was exempt from the militia so his family did not become a financial burden on the parish in his absence.

It is quite a skill to gather information about a person's military career. For some, such as Navy Officers, there are plenty of resources which are easy to use and understand. For others, such as WWI soldiers there may be little to go on. In these cases it can be useful to investigate more generic sources, such as war diaries and published regimental histories to understand what your ancestor may have been involved in. Visiting the regimental museum may also be of interest to you.

Many collections of military records have not survived. As mentioned earlier, many service records for WWI were lost in the bombing of WWII and some Merchant Navy muster rolls were destroyed in 1876. A large number of Tudor and Stuart Musters and Militia records do not survive and many of the annual militia lists compiled between 1757 and 1831 were destroyed.

Dorset Examples

After having seen photographs of my grandfather Thomas Osmond in military uniform, I sent a request to the Ministry of Defence to see what records, if any, had survived. I wasn't expecting to receive much, if anything, however, I was most surprised to discover that Thomas had enlisted as a private in the 4th Battalion of the Dorset Regiment in January 1926.

His enlistment form gives his occupation as a carter and states he was five feet five inches tall and weighed ten stone. Registered under Army Number 5722519, Thomas was in the Territorial Army for six years until 6 Jan 1932, during which time he attended summer training camps. On the 15 Mar 1938, aged thirty-four, Thomas re-enlisted into the same battalion. This time his enlistment form gives his occupation as a dairyman and his

31. Thomas Osmond during training.

weight had increased slightly to ten and a half stone. He served at home in England for just under two and a half years before being discharged in 1940, ruled as being permanently unfit for military service.

Militia lists held by Dorset History Centre and available on Ancestry show that on 23 Mar 1762 my sixth-great grandfather, Robert Squibb of Sutton Poyntz, was balloted to serve in the militia. A separate list shows that three weeks later Robert paid for a substitute named Nathaniel Haydon to take his place. The detail available in the militia lists varies. Robert's occupation is given as a servant.

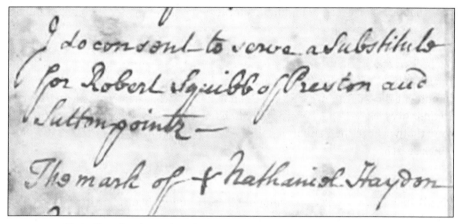

32. *Confirmation that Nathaniel Haydon served as a substitute for Robert Squibb.*

Some of my other ancestors who feature in militia lists include John Frampton of Swanage who is listed as being a shopkeeper and Andrew Puckett of Preston who was working as a shepherd. You may be lucky and find that extra details are given for your ancestor. My fifth-great grandfather, John Read, was balloted at the age of twenty in 1776 whilst residing at Sutton Poyntz. His height is given as five feet and five inches and his occupation stated as being a labourer. His 'single' marital status is recorded. Others on the page have the details of their substitute recorded, but John completed his service as requested.

CHAPTER 9
Newspapers

About the Record

Newspaper records are my personal favourite genealogical source. The possibilities of information that you may find are endless and can give a great insight into the lives of our ancestors, including criminal activity, accidents and obituaries. Many newspaper records are being digitised these days and made available online so these are generally easy to search.

By locating newspaper articles about our relatives, we can gain an insight into their characters, what their lives were like and what events were occurring in the parish at their time of life. Newspapers are one of the best sources to discover more about who our ancestors really were - knowing how they behaved will add context to their lives. Newspaper records are often fairly simple and easy to use, especially now that we have the benefit of being able to search newspapers online with one quick search.

Locating the Record

The British Library's online catalogue (http://explore.bl.uk) has listings of every newspaper published in the United Kingdom. Searching for the parish you are interested in can help you to find what papers may be of interest to you and you can then see what papers have yet to be uploaded to the British Newspaper Archive. Alternatively, have a look at *Local Newspapers 1750-1920* by Jeremy Gibson. Many of these for Dorset are available to view online.

The best websites for newspapers are the British Newspaper Archive, known as BNA (www.britishnewspaperarchive.co.uk) and FindMyPast, the latter of which has the records of BNA available on their Pro subscription. You may find it useful to know which Dorset newspapers have been digitised; this can be done via the filter functions on BNA and FindMyPast. For example, FindMyPast has editions of *Weymouth Telegram*, *Bridport News* and *Blandford Weekly News*. The earliest record currently dates back to 1748 in the *Sherborne Mercury*, although a majority of the records are from the 1800s and 1900s.

The best way to search is to enter your ancestor's name into the search box and then narrow this down accordingly. A rare name might not need to be filtered any further, but a majority will benefit from the addition of a place name or filtering by county to avoid searching through hundreds or thousands of records. You can also filter by date so you can just search between the years you know the person was alive to avoid viewing irrelevant records relating to others of the same name.

It is worth being aware when searching that not all reports will give an ancestor's full name. John Jones Smith may be recorded in one article under his full name but alternatively be found as John Smith, John J Smith, J J Smith or even simply Mr Smith. The latter is, of course, notoriously difficult to find but it can be done if the report mentions another identifiable term, such as their occupation or parish.

We have again the painful duty of recording a sudden death, if anything still more sudden than that of Mrs. Padley a fortnight ago. Mrs. Frampton, the wife of Mr. Frampton, butcher, in Market-street, formerly a Miss Keynes, on Monday, as usual, went about her domestic duties and served in the shop in the early part of the morning in apparently good health. About 11

33. An article from 1863 about the death of Mrs Frampton of Poole. Neither her, nor her husband are named but their street address, his occupation and her maiden name are given.

The Times has a fantastic archive website of their old editions. The London Gazette featured public notices such as bankruptcy and military awards for people based all over the country. You can search their archives for free at www.thegazette. co.uk.

When you have located an entry about your ancestor, note the name of the newspaper and its date so you can refer to this again in the future if needed. Save a copy of the image for your records and carefully read the article to make sure you have extracted every piece of useful information.

With a majority of records there is a general interest to view the record in person rather than online. With newspapers this tends to be of less value, but if you wish to view a paper copy, contact local libraries to see what they hold.

Values of the Record

The values of newspaper records are so great that it is impossible to list them all. Everybody will be able to find some of their ancestors in newspaper articles, but not every individual ancestor will feature. Men feature more commonly than women and are often easier to locate in the source if their occupation or residence is mentioned.

Newspaper articles regarding criminal trials are amongst the most useful, often recording the words our ancestors spoke in court, known as *verbatim*. They may appear as the defendant, the accuser, a witness or an official. Reports on Coroners' Inquests can be equally useful, particularly as the original reports have often been destroyed. The article will mention the key points of the coroner's findings and can help the reader to understand the circumstances of their ancestor's death.

The columns of births, marriages and deaths are obviously useful too and can help us find the relevant GRO certificate, as well as providing extra details. There are examples of stillbirths featuring in the birth columns, causes of death being stated in the death columns and father's names listed in the marriage columns. There are often separate articles on local weddings. These can name bridesmaids and best man, give details as to flower arrangements and chosen music and quote where the happy couple went on honeymoon. These are lovely pieces of information which would never be found on a certificate.

BIRTHS.

PARHAM.—July 11, at Corfe Mullen, the wife of Mr. W. Parham, of a daughter, stillborn.

SHORT.—July 4, at the Bank, Isle of Portland, the wife of Mr. J. J. R. Short, of a son.

LYS.—July 13, at Bere Regis, Dorset, the wife of F. D. Lys, Esq., surgeon, of a son.

34. An extract from a births' column from Dorset County Chronicle 1863.
Note that the first child was stillborn and may not feature in other records.

Other articles may include obituaries detailing an ancestor's life, educational achievements, business advertisements and interviews with people about a notable event, such as reaching a special birthday or anniversary. *The London Gazette* is excellent at providing us with details of military and civil service awards. An article dating 19 Oct 1965 details how Constable Kenneth Middleton Pearce of Wool was awarded the British Empire Medal for rescuing a man stuck on a cliff edge. *The London Gazette* also details bankruptcy cases, such as in an article dating 8 Nov 1755 when Thomas and Joseph Tuckett of Piddletown (now Puddletown) were declared bankrupt.

Reports of major and minor accidents are common features in newspapers. There have been very few fatal train accidents in the county, largely because the network was smaller compared with other counties; however, if your ancestor was involved in an accident, details will be found in local newspapers, as well as national editions if it was serious enough to deem worth publishing elsewhere. Accidents that occurred in other counties may feature your Dorset ancestors, such as the 1876 Radstock collision between a Bath-Bournemouth train and Wimborne-Bath train which claimed fifteen lives. You may also come across articles detailing accidents in factories, on the roads or at sea.

As well as the articles which name our ancestors, it can also be interesting to read pieces of local news about the town or village where your ancestor lived. There may be details of village fetes, royal visits, weather events or pageants which may of general interest. Events such as these can help to pad out an ancestor's life story if you are writing their biography and information is scarce. You may discover that their village was badly flooded, suffered a disastrous fire or experienced a localised pandemic. Events such as the Great Fire of Blandford in 1731, the Great Storm of 1824 which caused huge damage to Fleet and Chiswell and the September 1940 bombing of Sherborne would undoubtedly have touched the lives of everyone in those parishes.

When searching articles for your ancestors you should always be aware that you may not like what you find. Whilst there may be tales of heroism, there may also be accounts of a less favourable nature. Newspapers used to be particularly graphic about accidents that occurred, such as those involving farm machinery or trains. This is more upsetting to read if we are researching people closer to home.

Limitations of the Record

As remains the case today, we need to be aware that newspaper reports may be biased, untruthful and exaggerated. Details that witnesses give in court may be swayed in order to find the defendant innocent or guilty. Obituaries may also be written in great favour of the deceased - and with false information stated. Newspaper records can be a great first step in a particular line of research, but then you must follow up to try and verify what you have found. For example, it may be possible to find surviving court records which give a more rounded picture of an event.

Newspaper pages are searched using a technique known as 'optical character recognition' where the pages are read digitally, rather than relying on a person to transcribe the record word by word. Whilst this is a much quicker process, it is not perfect. Letters may be read incorrectly so if you are searching for an exact name, this may not appear in the search results if the digitisation process read a letter wrongly. This is more likely to occur with older newspaper copies, where the writing is often thicker and harder for a computer to read.

While researching your Dorset ancestors, it can be useful to filter the results to show only those from the county. Bear in mind that you may miss articles of relevance if you do this, with many featuring in articles from neighbouring counties, as well as further afield if the news was particularly noteworthy.

You will find newspaper records for your ancestors from the nineteenth century onwards, however, anything before that is unlikely. The first British newspaper, the *Weekly News*, was published in London from 1662, whilst the origins of the *London Gazette* go back to 1665. Local newspapers only developed on a wide scale from the 1830s. Be aware when searching local newspaper records that the names of newspapers often changed over time, as did the area that they covered.

Dorset Examples

My fourth great-grandfather, William Read, was born in Sutton Poyntz in 1781 and died in 1847, making it less likely he would appear in a newspaper article as they became more prevalent after his death. What makes the newspaper article that features him even more unusual is that he is not named in it and the article dates from 6 Apr 1934, nearly ninety years after his death!

> He mentioned that his grandfather on his mother's side was interned in a French prison for 21 years during the wars with France. When he was released, and returned home, he " looked like a wild man," by reason of his beard having been allowed to grow unchecked during those many years.

35. *The article mentioning William Read, albeit not by name.*

By tracing articles of more distant family members, I was able to find an article that mentioned him in the *Western Gazette*, but naming him as the subject's *grandfather on his mother's side*. The article goes on to state that William *was interned in a French prison for 21 years during the wars with France*. This certainly helped to explain his absence from records up until his marriage in 1816 at the age of thirty-five; however, aside from this article, no other proof has been found of his imprisonment. I do not doubt that he was imprisoned in France and there are certainly records of William Read's being held captive there, but unfortunately they do not give enough information to identify him positively. My main doubt is the length of time he was held there. Even if he married as soon as he arrived home, he would have been aged fourteen when he was captured. It is likely he would have known his wife for a short time at least before getting married and it is questionable as to what age William would have been when sent to France to fight. Common sense and a little research are sometimes needed to gain the truth behind the newspaper article.

Another example which highlights the usefulness of newspaper articles is the marriage notice of my grandparents, Dorothy Jessie Taylor and Thomas Osmond, at Broadmayne in the *Western Gazette* on 11 Aug 1939. This notes the hymns that were sung, gives details of the bride's and bridesmaid's dresses and that Thomas' best man was Dorothy's uncle.

Dorothy's mother, Susan Eunice Hatcher, features in a somewhat more disturbing article in the *Taunton Courier* on 27 Sep 1916. Susan was working as a servant in a residence where the cook secretly gave birth to a baby that she

BROADMAYNE

BANK HOLIDAY WEDDING.—The wedding of Mr. Thomas Osmond, second son of the late Mr. and Mrs. Osmond, to Miss Dorothy Jesse Taylor, eldest daughter of Mrs. Quinton, took place on Bank Holiday, the Rev. A. C. Board (rector) and Rev. E. S. Daniell (Litton Cheney) officiating. The hymns were "Lead us, Heavenly Father" and "Thine for ever, God of Love." Mr. Henry James Hatcher (uncle of the bride) was "best man," and gave the bride away, and Miss Daisy Joan Spencer was bridesmaid. The bride wore a white bridal satin dress, with wreath and veil, and carried a sheaf of lilies. The bridesmaid was in a blue satin dress, with head-dress to match, and carried a bouquet of pink and white carnations.

36. Notice of the marriage of Thomas Osmond and Dorothy Taylor.

subsequently killed. The article notes there were questions as to whether Susan was aware of the incident or if she helped to conceal the evidence, however, she was cleared. It is an example of how graphic accounts could be, as the article is a rather gruesome read. It also shows why we shouldn't always limit our searches to Dorset; despite this incident occurring in Upwey in Dorset the article was published in Taunton, Somerset.

CHAPTER 10
Maps

About the Record

Maps can tell us so much more than just what the geography of a place used to be. They can show us where our ancestors lived, how much land they owned, who their neighbours were and how close they lived to parish amenities and other family members. Viewing a variety of maps for one area can show us how the place has changed over time and how different villages and towns grew with an ever-increasing, sprawling population. They can help us to understand the changes to a parish that particular ancestors would have witnessed, such as the building of a new church or the merging of two villages into one. This chapter will not only look at maps but also the relevant documents that we find attached to them, such as tithe apportionments and surveys.

Tithe maps are some of the most useful and easiest to access thanks to their upload onto the Ancestry website. Tithes were a type of tax payment whereby one tenth of produce and goods was paid to the parish church, regardless of whether a person was Anglican or not. Due to several issues with collecting tithes, such as refusal to pay and the difficulty in paying certain tithes (such as how to donate a tenth of honey produce), the practice was altered so that monetary payment was collected instead. The Tithe Commutation Act of 1836 led to tithe maps and apportionments being created for each tithe district (usually a parish) so that this new monetary collection system could be formally established. The apportionments are the written records associated with the map providing the names of the landowners and occupiers.

Enclosure maps often have a similar appearance to tithe maps and you may be lucky to find both existing for the same parish. Land used to be held in much smaller areas than the fields we see today; land was often in strips, which was deemed not to be the most profitable way of using it. Parishes could therefore undergo 'enclosure' via an Act of Parliament which transformed the land into what we see today - large fields surrounded by hedges and fences. When this process was simplified by the General Enclosure Act of 1801, the process became much more popular. Maps that were created at the time of enclosure show who owned each plot of land, along with the new field layout.

Some of the oldest surviving maps of an area are estate maps. These were drawn up on behalf of landowners who wished to value their property, have evidence of the extent of this land and to help with establishing rents for those who lived within the estate. There are many more contemporary examples of these also.

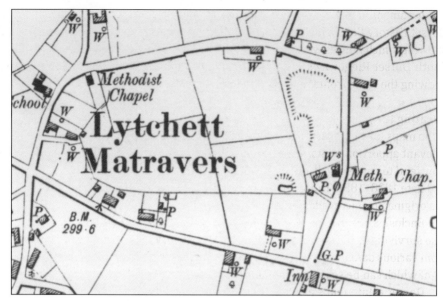

37. An OS map of 1900 for Lytchett Matravers. Note that the key buildings are annotated, including the school, chapels and an inn.

The most reliable and accurate maps are those of the Ordnance Survey (OS). First established in 1791, their maps were not mass produced until 1914. As Great Britain's official map creator, the company has high standards and their maps are well known for their detail and accuracy.

Maps have always been created for various purposes and as genealogists we have to bear this reasoning in mind. Maps showing builders' diagrams, public utility plans and fire insurance schedules can all be used by family historians. Detailed maps were created by engineers, architects and builders to show plans for new services, such as railways, new housing estates and improvements to water works. Fire insurance companies held maps showing properties that were covered by their policies, with the accompanying documentation giving information about the householder.

Two more recent records from the 1900s are the National Farm Survey from the 1940s and the Lloyd George Domesday Maps from 1910 -1915. The National Farm Survey is of great interest to Dorset because of its rich farming history and is a great record for people to research their parents and grandparents. The survey was undertaken during WWII due to agricultural issues at the time and assessed each farm's land use, fertility, size and utility provision. The Lloyd George Domesday records, also referred to as Inland Revenue Valuations, were made after the 1910 Finance Act introduced a new tax on property sales meaning each house had to be assessed and mapped.

A number of other more unique maps to specific areas exist. Examples held at Dorset History Centre include a map of Blandford Forum made after the 1731 fire showing which houses were damaged and which properties survived, a map of the South Dorset Ridgeway's archaeological sites and a map drawn by John Ogilby showing the route from Weymouth to London, dated 1675.

Locating the Record

Tithe maps for Dorset are easiest to access via the Ancestry website, along with the relevant apportionments. Three copies of the original documents were created so they tend to survive well, either at Dorset History Centre or The National Archives, and date 1838 -1854. The apportionments are transcribed alongside each map, with the original images available on The Genealogist.

Enclosure records are held at The National Archives in Series CP 43, with some also surviving in county record offices. Dorset History Centre has a good collection from various dates, such as from Buckhorn Weston in 1804 and Batcombe in 1863, all of which can be searched via their catalogue.

Dorset estate maps are held in a variety of locations including The National Archives, Dorset History Centre and in private hands. Dorset History Centre holds the 1750 estate map of Kingston Russell and one for Corfe Castle dating 1844, along with many others. Both the National Farm Survey and Lloyd George's Domesday records are held at The National Archives. The records of the National Farm Survey are held in MAF 32 whilst the maps are in MAF 73. The Lloyd George Domesday field books are the most used in Series IR 58, with plans at IR 121 and valuation books at IR 91. The records from the Lloyd George survey are currently being digitised by The Genealogist website. Whilst counties such as Buckinghamshire and Middlesex are available now, Dorset has yet to be digitised.

Dorset History Centre also holds several fire insurance maps, public utility maps and builders' plans. It is worth searching the catalogue for maps of your parish of interest to see what survives, including those more unique maps which can often be the most interesting. The National Archives also holds many of this latter category so do check on their Discovery catalogue for their holdings. Ordnance Survey maps are held at Dorset History Centre, the National Archives and the British Library. There is also a large collection of maps online at the National Library of Scotland, which covers England, Scotland and Wales (https://maps.nls.uk).

Values of the Record

Tithe maps cover around seventy per cent of Dorset so there is a good chance you will find a map for your parish of interest. The maps clearly show the road layout through the parish which in many cases is recognisable today, with each plot of land subject to paying tithes clearly marked with a boundary and numbered. This number corresponds to the apportionment book which lists the occupiers name and landowners' names, so it is easy to see which plots belonged to your ancestor and where they lived. The apportionments also give a brief description of the plot (such as garden or arable land), the size of the plot and the monetary tithe payment the occupier is due to pay.

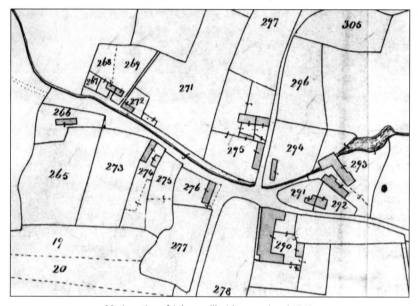

38. *A section of Askerswell's tithe map dated 1845.*

Enclosure maps are particularly useful to those researching land-owning ancestors. The map will show the extent of the land that their ancestor owned and its placement in the parish. There is often a good amount of geographical detail, and notable buildings are usually included such as the village church. Builders' plans and public utility maps can also show details of the geography of an area and can offer an insight into how a parish looked before and after a major development that may have affected your ancestor's life. They are generally fairly accurate but Ordnance Survey maps are by far the most reliable for accuracy and scale.

Estate maps vary considerably in their detail. Some are excellent, showing every property in the area with geographical details highlighted, including field names, rivers and barrows. Details from associated records with the maps are very helpful to us. The National Farm Survey gives the farmer's name along with the number of employees they had. The Lloyd George Domesday field books give both the property occupier and owners' names along with the address and other property details, such as its estimated value and amount of rent due.

Maps really do bring history to life; there is much information in one attractive image. They are most useful when compared with contemporary maps of the same area to see how the area has changed. Use them to help with your understanding of the parish that your ancestor lived in and make sure you examine the records carefully to extract as much useful information as possible.

Limitations of the Record
Tithe maps vary in quality and detail. Sometimes a parish did not contain any land subject to tithe payment so no map was produced in these cases. Enclosure maps similarly had no standardised format, resulting in a wide array of quality and sometimes no buildings were drawn either making the map harder to relate to today. Not all parishes were enclosed, so again, there will not be a map for every parish. Estate maps also vary in quality but are also more likely to only show a small area of a parish, depending on what was relevant to the estate and the purpose of the map being created.

As with most genealogical sources, these will not cover everyone. The National Farm Survey only covers agricultural property and land, whilst the Lloyd George survey and tithe maps only name the chief occupier, rather than all who reside in the dwelling. The amount of detail in public utility maps and builders' plans will depend on their reason for creation. For example, if a map was created to demonstrate the placing of a new railway line, only the area affected is likely to be drawn, rather than a whole parish. It is not guaranteed that properties will feature on each map. It is also fairly rare to find fire insurance plans for rural areas, with most showing towns and cities.

Whilst Ordnance Survey maps are highly rated for their attention to detail and precision, their use can be limited if used on their own. Some buildings are clearly marked, but others are harder to decipher and pin down such as a property in a row of terraced houses where your ancestor lived. They also have no written documentation attached, such as householders' names, as this was not needed for their original purpose. Ordnance Survey maps are best used when comparing them with other maps of the same area. The map-viewer on The Genealogist website is excellent for this, showing two maps on top of one another of your choice, so you can see easily how one area has changed over time.

Maps are always a snapshot in time. It is essential to discover when the map was produced, but be aware that even if the map shows your ancestor owning a particular plot of land, the maps alone cannot tell you how long your ancestor owned the plot. It may be that it was only owned for a few months, or perhaps they owned the land for generations. Further sources will need to be used to track the ownership. This may mean perusing a variety of maps for the same parish or tracking down deeds or wills which relate to land ownership. The same is true for property occupation.

Dorset Examples

I have found Tithe Maps to be particularly useful for my family tree. Most of those listed are male, although there are quite a few females too, generally widows who have been left property by their deceased husbands but not always as my example shows. My fourth great-grandmother, Hannah Osment, resided in Sutton Poyntz all her life. She never married, had two children and several brushes with the law. Despite this, she managed to own her property within the parish. The 1838 Tithe Apportionment for Sutton Poyntz, available on The Genealogist website, shows that Hannah owned the property she occupied, namely a cottage and garden. The size of her property is given as four perches, which equates to about 100 square metres and the assessment shows she did not have to pay tithes. Her plot number is ninety-five.

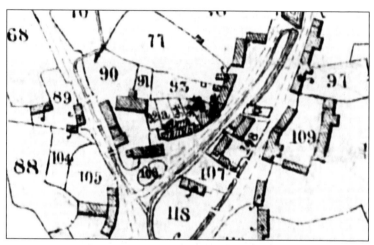

39. 1838 tithe map for Sutton Poyntz. Hannah's property is number 95, situated below number 93.

Using this number to look at the tithe map, we can see that her property is one of the smallest in the parish situated near the centre of the village not far from the stream. Interestingly, two plots to her left is John Puckett, the father of her son Thomas born in 1824. It is certainly interesting to see the close proximity within which they lived but raises many questions, such as what relationship did Thomas have with his father? How did John's wife feel about them living so close to the woman with whom he had an affair? Whilst maps cannot answer these questions, they certainly are good at provoking extra thought and lines of enquiry.

Using Ordnance Survey maps in different ways can also help your research. As mentioned before, they contain no information about householders and the only named buildings are those which are notable in the parish, such as the church or farmsteads. This can be of help to situate your ancestor's residence. My great-grandmother, Susan Eunice Hatcher, is listed in the 1901 census as living in Bincombe, near the school. Census records frequently do not give the house numbers of properties, mainly because they didn't exist back then, so looking at the route the enumerator took can sometimes also help you to locate their residence.

Knowing from the census that Susan was aged four and living near the school tells me she had a very short commute as a pupil. Looking at the Ordnance Survey map from the same period helps me to locate her and her family. The OS map clearly shows Bincombe School towards the north of the village. There are only three properties close to the school so Susan is most likely to have lived in one of those.

When looking further at the map, it shows that the parish church is at the opposite end of the village, meaning she would have to walk through the village to get to Sunday service. Her father, Walter, worked at East Farm which is also shown on the map, again at the opposite end of the village. Even though an ancestor's property is not always clearly marked on an Ordnance Survey map, knowing where key buildings are can help us paint a picture of their daily lives within a parish.

40. *Early 1900s OS map of Bincombe showing the school, church and East Farm.*

CHAPTER 11
Criminal and Court Records

About the Record

Records surrounding criminality are of great interest to family historians. Your ancestor may feature in these records as an alleged criminal, a victim or a witness. Either way, the records can open our eyes to the living conditions at the time and personal characteristics of our ancestors. My great-great grandfather, Alexander Taylor, was a habitual criminal and was described as a 'gang-leader' in the late 1800s. Newspaper records of court cases report him as being unemployed, lazy and violent. Whilst he is not a relative to be particularly proud of, the number of times he committed crimes leads to many records being left behind, which help to paint a colourful picture of his life and that of his long-suffering wife Alice.

Minor criminal cases were heard at Petty Sessions and Quarter Sessions, such as petty theft and assault; the more major cases were heard at Assizes, such as murder and rape, although there was some overlap. Quarter Sessions records are often fairly vague, briefly outlining the offence, the names of the parties involved and the jury's verdict. An early punishment meted out here involved being held in the village stocks or in a parish 'cage'. Records from Quarter Sessions include minute books listing those in attendance, order books detailing verdicts and sentences, and session rolls holding witness statements, recognizances and jury lists. Quarter Sessions were presided over by Justices of the Peace who also heard cases regarding non-payment of child support in bastardy cases, refusal to pay tithes and apprenticeship issues. In Dorset, the sessions were mostly heard at Blandford, Bridport, Shaftesbury and Sherborne, although each session could look at issues from anywhere within the county, and they date from 1625. Quarter Sessions were not only used for criminal proceedings. Amongst their records you can also find licences, rate payers' lists, registration of new charities and matters relating to civil engineering and upkeep such as roads and bridges.

Assize records are more detailed, largely due to the more serious nature of the offences. Assize courts were organised in circuits, with judges moving between locations in the circuits to hear cases. Dorset was in the Western Circuit, including the Poole area. Records produced from assize courts include depositions (witness statements) and court minute books which give a case summary and recognizances, where a person agreed to do something before the court. You may also find calendars of prisoners which are lists of alleged criminals, not all of whom were found guilty as the list was made before the trial occurred.

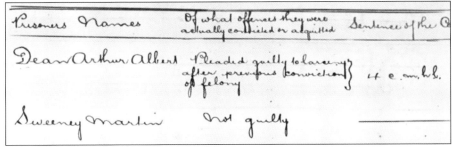

41. *Quarter Sessions order book dating 1890 from Dorchester showing Arthur Albert Dean sentenced to 4 months hard labour for larceny whilst Martin Sweeney was found not guilty.*

If an ancestor was believed to have committed a moral sin, rather than a crime, they could be brought before the ecclesiastical courts run by the Church. Offences tried there included adultery, working on a Sunday and defamation. The parish churchwarden had to present those whom he believed to be guilty to the court that could then order a minor punishment after evidence was heard. Any minor criminal acts committed within manor boundaries could also be heard by the manorial courts, as discussed in the Manorial Records chapter of this book.

The Prison Service has only been run by the Home Office since 1877. The Home Office Register of Criminals for England and Wales notes the person's offence and sentence if found guilty. Prison registers note convicts in order of their admission. Prior to the nineteenth century, imprisonment was rarely used as towns used prisons mainly to hold debtors or those awaiting trial rather than as a form of punishment in itself. Punishments included transportation from 1615, flogging and hanging.

In the nineteenth century, there were gaols at Shaftesbury, Blandford, Poole, Wareham, Portland, Weymouth, Dorchester, Bridport and Lyme Regis. There were further local lock-ups at Cerne Abbas, Corfe Castle, Gillingham, Okeford Fitzpaine, Stalbridge and Swanage. These lock-ups could hold people on a short-term basis, perhaps only for a day or two, whilst the authorities decided whether to release them or investigate their crime further.

Between 1800 and 1964, 4304 people were executed in England and Wales. Only thirty-three of these were in Dorset and all of these executions were carried out in Dorchester. The last execution in the county was in 1941 when twenty-one-year-old David Jennings was hanged for the murder of Albert Farley in Dorchester. Earlier examples include seventy-four-year-old John Foot who was executed in 1801 for stealing a lamb from Buckland Newton and sixteen-year-old Sylvester Wilkins of Bridport who was hanged in 1833 for arson. Prior to 1800 executions took place elsewhere in the county. For example, William King and Ben Fluel were executed opposite Blandford Forum town hall in 1741 after being found guilty of robbery.

Dorset had many smugglers due to its coastal location. Smuggling occurred all along the Dorset coast from Lyme Regis to Weymouth to the Isle of Purbeck to Bournemouth and was at its peak between 1700 and 1830. Smugglers were well practised at keeping a look-out and hiding from the authorities, such as the parish constable, revenue officer or Coastguard, however, many were still caught and imprisoned. They illegally handled tobacco, tea, alcohol such as wine and brandy, fabrics such as satin, coffee and cocoa amongst other goods. Smugglers were part of well-organised gangs and, despite the often romanticised view of them their lives were often surrounded with violence and deceit. If you find a smuggler in your family tree, you may discover that they found themselves injured, perhaps through gunshot wounds or through an accident whilst navigating the network of tunnels they had built in the cliffs.

Locating the Record

The easiest way to find information regarding an ancestor's criminal trial is to search newspaper records online, such as the British Newspaper Archive or FindMyPast. A name search and their place of residence can bring up results detailing the alleged crime and later court appearances. Major crimes, such as murder, are more likely to feature in national newspapers – and even the more minor crimes can be sometimes found in national papers if editors deemed them to be of interest to readers.

There are many court and criminal records available online. Records of Quarter Sessions are held at Dorset History Centre and are available online at Ancestry dating 1625-1905. Dorset History Centre holds petty sessions records and Dorchester Prison registers 1812-1962.

The more serious the crime, the more likely your ancestor's criminal records will be found at the National Archives, the repository which holds assizes records. The Home Office Register of Criminals is held at TNA in series HO 27 and is also available online at The Genealogist, Ancestry and FindMyPast. TNA also holds records relating to transportation, including convicts transported to Australia 1787-1870 in HO 11. These are again available online at The Genealogist and Ancestry. The Register of Habitual Criminals is held at PCOM 2/404 and dates 1869 -1876, noting over 12,000 convictions and the last prison where the criminals were held. TNA also hold details and personal correspondence regarding those sentenced to death in PCOM 8-9, Criminal Entry Books at SP44 and assizes records after 1858 in ASSI 1-54 amongst many others.

Dorset prison records feature in Ancestry's collection 'UK, Prison Commission Records 1770-1951' and FindMyPast's holding of 'England & Wales, Crime, Prisons & Punishment 1770-1935'. Ancestry also has a great Dorset specific collection including Dorset Convict Transportation Records for 1724-1791, Dorchester Prison

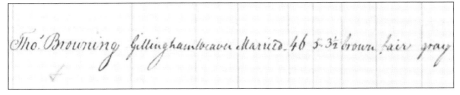

42. *Extract from Dorchester Prison register dated 1807 showing 46-year-old married weaver Thomas Browning of Gillingham. He was found guilty of assault and sentenced to prison for one month.*

Admission and Discharge Registers 1782-1860, Dorset Calendars of Prisoners 1854 -1904 and Dorset Jury Lists 1825 -1921.

There are many other websites you may be interested to view. Blacksheep Ancestors (www.blacksheepancestors.com) holds many interesting notes of previous criminal convictions, the Australian National Archives (www.naa.gov.au) will be of interest to those whose ancestors were transported to Australia and the Old Bailey Trials site (www.oldbaileyonline.org) contains transcripts of court proceedings from the Old Bailey.

Values of the Record

Discovering that an ancestor was guilty of a crime or was a victim of a criminal act can give an insight into their lives. Perhaps your ancestor was found guilty of repeated thefts because they were unemployed and trying to provide for their family? If your ancestor was a victim of theft, records might reveal some of the items they possessed and indicate their wealth, status and occupation if the item was used for their work. Where an ancestor was imprisoned, this can explain why they were missing from their household on census night or explain a gap between births of their children if they were imprisoned for several years. Where prisoners were included in the census, they were often listed by just their initials rather than their full names which can make them hard to find.

If you find your ancestor was transported, this can explain why they suddenly go missing from the Dorset records. The usual terms of transportation were for seven years, fourteen years or for life; some did not return home, with many remaining in Australia. The journey to get there was harsh and many died en-route. You may find in the records that your relative was hanged as punishment or died whilst incarcerated, the documentation of which should tell you their date of death.

It is not uncommon to find relationships listed in criminal records. It may be that a husband and wife were both found guilty of child abandonment, a mother and daughter may be found guilty of assault and blasphemy after a public family feud or a woman may be called to give evidence in defence of, or against, their partner. As well as looking at the 'criminal' ancestor, consider the impact that the event had on their family. When a husband was imprisoned, the wife and children were generally left without financial support. Even if a person was found guilty of a minor crime, their family name may have been tarnished locally resulting in the family moving to another parish.

Prison registers can give the prisoner's name, age, religion, date of entry into prison and their sentence. Entries often give a physical description including hair colour, height and any tattoos or scars. Certain entries in the Register of Habitual Criminals and some prison records include a photograph of the convicted criminal which may be the only surviving photograph of your ancestor. Newspaper records reporting criminal trials can be amongst some of the more detailed reports and may include quotations from your ancestor. They may be pleading innocence or detailing the crime in their own terms. Whatever they are quoted as saying, it is often the only time we get to 'hear' our ancestors' voices and get a sense of their character.

BOROUGH PETTY SESSIONS, Monday.—Before the Mayor (Mr. T. H. Bennett) and Mr. C. Pond.—*Hannah Knight*, a married woman, residing in East-street, Blandford, was brought up in custody charged with attempting to commit a felony. The prisoner was apprehended on Saturday afternoon in Mr. Vine's shop, where she had gone ostensibly to make purchases. Whilst there she was observed by one of the assistants to put a black straw hat under her dress, and on being accused denied having taken anything. A policeman was sent for, but previous to his arrival prisoner took from under her dress four pairs of stockings, the hat, and a small cotton fancy necktie. She was at once [given into custody. The magistrates remanded prisouer.

43. Article from 1874 stating Hannah Knight of Blandford was seen to steal several items of clothing which she denied doing.

Limitations of the Record

It is tempting to label our ancestors as bad people if they were found guilty of committing a crime. As with today, life is rarely that black and white and we should not label our ancestors as good or bad based on whether or not they committed a crime. In some cases it is fair to gain a certain opinion of our ancestors, particularly if they were found guilty of murder, rape or abuse. However, where they committed a single act of something like assault, theft or fraud, try to discover more about their lives and the possible reasoning behind committing these acts. They may have been acting in self-defence, stealing food to feed a starving family or they may have been innocent all along, even if found guilty. Any witness statements that have been given will give you a clearer idea of the character of your criminal ancestor.

The limitation of many criminal records is that the reasoning behind the crime cannot be found. In many cases it is also not possible to be certain whether or not they were in fact guilty or innocent. Even our most seemingly law-abiding ancestors may have committed a crime only to escape justice for it. The reliability of witness statements should always be questioned, with many contradicting each other. Where a good amount of documentation has survived, try to gather this together and treat it like a modern day investigation. Look at the motives for the criminal, victim and witnesses. Remember that today we also have a greater understanding of how mental health and mental capacity can have an impact upon people involved in criminal activity in a way that was not well understood in the past.

It is advisable to question everything you read. Whilst certain information such as dates of trials or imprisonment is more factual, other details are not clear. Those accused may lie about their place of residence or give an alias, making it hard to trace them through the records. Newspapers often sensationalised crimes, as they still do today. 'Facts' may be exaggerated and characters may be smeared without proper grounds. People were often interested in female criminals who may be portrayed as negative influences in society if they were poor or convicted of prostitution.

Some research may need to be done in order to understand the gravity of the crime that your ancestor committed on the date they were convicted. The usual example looks at sheep stealing which used to carry the death penalty at assizes but over time was treated much less severely at Quarter Sessions. You may have two ancestors generations apart found guilty of the same crime but punished very differently.

Not all criminal records have survived. Many earlier parish constables' records have been lost, early petty sessions records tend not to survive and many assizes records were destroyed. A majority of criminal records have not yet been digitized or transcribed, meaning a trip to the archives is necessary. At times it can be hard to understand certain legal terms used in the past, so make a note of anything you do not understand to research later. Quarter Sessions order books from the 1600s are mostly written in Latin and can be hard to read.

Dorset Examples

My fifth great-grandfather, Jacob Naile (1762-1839) of Toller Porcorum, did not leave much documentation behind in his lifetime. Jacob was found guilty of *assaulting and wounding* another person in 1789 when he was twenty-seven. On the 8 May he was sentenced to one month's imprisonment at Dorchester at the Summer Assizes.

Whilst this incident was no doubt a bad experience for Jacob, for me as a genealogist the fact that he committed this crime is actually very useful! For a man who otherwise left a small paper trail, Jacob can be seen in the Dorchester Gaol

44. Jacob's entry in Dorchester Prison's register for 1789.

prisoner register, held by Dorset History Centre and available on Ancestry. This extremely detailed register tells us that Jacob was 5 feet 10 inches tall, had light-coloured hair and grey eyes. It is also noted that Jacob had a bruise to the right of his nose and a scar above his beard on the left-hand side. This paints quite a picture of Jacob's physical appearance that would otherwise have remained lost to history.

Another crime from the same page on the register is that of James Dominey of Iwerne Minster who was found guilty of stealing a brass kettle at the same Assizes session as Jacob. James was not imprisoned. Instead, he received a public whipping in Dorchester, no doubt a painful and humiliating experience for James. He is listed as being 5 feet 10 inches tall with brown hair, a pale complexion and dark eyes.

When my fourth great-grandmother, Hannah Osment of Sutton Poyntz, was found guilty of smuggling on 22 Dec 1838, none of her physical characteristics are recorded, unlike most others on the same page of the prison admission register. Hannah was imprisoned for six months and was released on time on 21 Jun 1839. Her behaviour is described as orderly, but little other information is given. Other examples from the same register as Hannah include Matthew Pitcher, a fisherman of Tyneham, found guilty of poaching and sentenced to two month's hard labour and Robert Ames, a baker of Milborne St Andrew, found guilty of assaulting a policeman and sentenced to six month's imprisonment.

45. Extract from the Dorchester Prison register showing Hannah Osment's
(written here as Osmond) entry for smuggling in 1838.

CHAPTER 12
Memorial Inscriptions

About the Record

The value of memorial inscriptions is often reduced to a short paragraph in genealogy books, with minimal information on how they can help you as a family historian. I feel they deserve their own chapter in this book as they can be so crucial to genealogical research and are at risk of being overlooked. In short, memorial inscriptions are text featured on the headstones where our ancestors were buried. These can vary from a simple headstone featuring the deceased's name and year of death to a very detailed headstone, naming several members of the same family, their dates of birth, dates of death, occupations and relationships to each other. Most likely, the detail on your ancestor's headstones will feature somewhere between the two.

The first step is to discover where your ancestor is buried. This can usually be done using the burial registers at Dorset History Centre which are now available on Ancestry. You could also search websites, such as Find a Grave and Deceased Online, where people upload images of headstones with transcriptions. You can search by name or by parish. See what work has been completed with headstone transcriptions and photography in the parish where you live, as well as where your ancestors lived. By spending an hour in your local churchyard and uploading the photos to Find a Grave, you could help someone break down a brick wall. I have uploaded hundreds of photographs and always target the stones which are looking particularly weathered in an attempt to salvage the information that is written upon them.

You may like to record the type of memorial that marks your ancestor's grave. *Ledgers* are horizontal stone memorials that are found lying flat on the ground and are sometimes seen with double panels, one each for a husband and wife. If you believe your ancestor has a ledger as a memorial, be careful to check its surroundings to see if it was installed this way or if it in fact was originally erected as an upright headstone that has since fallen. A ledger is generally much squarer than a headstone. Another memorial often seen in churchyards is a chest tomb, a box-like stone feature, which may feature text or imagery on the side of it. The body was always buried below ground, never within the square tomb itself. Tombs were only affordable to the wealthier classes within the parish. If your ancestor was less well-off, you may find their memorial is simply their initials on a small upright stone. This is known as a grave marker; these sometimes survive in front of a headstone that was erected afterwards and is then known as a footstone.

46. *Memorials at Chaldon Herring/East Chaldon.*

A majority of memorials within churchyards and cemeteries are simply known as headstones and are the usual upright stones. Many of our ancestors would have been given a simple wooden marker for their grave which will since have rotted away. A small minority of burials can be found inside parish churches. These belong to the wealthier families within a parish, such as the elaborate seventeenth-century tombs belonging to Sir John Fitzjames and Sir Thomas Winston in Longburton church.

Locating the Record

Undoubtedly, the best way to record memorial inscriptions is in person. If you are able to visit the churchyard or cemetery yourself, it is most definitely worth having a look. You may notice a feature on the headstone that wasn't clear on the photograph or discover the headstones of other ancestors close by whose details have yet to be uploaded to a website. It is also of general interest to visit the churchyard to see where your ancestors attended church and where events, such as baptism, marriage and burial services were held.

If you are unable to visit in person, there are several online resources that may be of help. The websites of Find a Grave (www.findagrave.com) and Deceased Online (www.deceasedonline.com) both offer a selection of memorial inscriptions of select parishes, often with a photograph uploaded. The number of burials that have been uploaded varies according to parish. For example, Gillingham has the names of over 600 people buried there whereas Todber does not currently feature at all. Dorset OPC (www.opcdorset.org) has a select number of memorial inscriptions, including those for Todber. This shows that you should always check every available source to see what has been uploaded.

FindMyPast has a collection of over 120,000 memorial inscriptions from Dorset parishes. This collection was provided by both the Dorset Family History Society and the Somerset and Dorset Family History Society. The details given here are terrific. As an example, a transcription from Winterborne Came details that George Osmond died on 12 Jul 1834 aged fifty-five and was the father of Walter Osmond. The denomination is given as Church of England and the type of monument is stated as being a headstone cross. The earliest inscription dates from 1467 - a plaque belonging to Alicia Whitewood, the wife of John of Langton Long. Whilst there are no photographs, these transcriptions are the next best thing due to their great detail. Lists of rectors from parish churches also feature where brass plaques situated inside parish churches have been transcribed. If your ancestor is found in any of these transcriptions on FindMyPast, it is advisable to contact the Family History Societies to see if they have any further details, such as burial information or a map of the cemetery.

Ancestry's collection 'Records of the Removal of Graves and Tombstones, 1601-1980' includes named graves of people whose burial sites were relocated. For Dorset, these include Poole's Unitarian Church Burial Ground on Hill Street, Shaftesbury's Holy Trinity Burial Ground and Weymouth's Bury Street Burial Ground. For Shaftesbury, only the deceased's name and year of death is given. For Poole and Weymouth, the whole memorial inscription is recorded, where the stone has survived.

"Underneath in a wall'd grave are deposited the remains of Tabatha Mary Baynes who died November 26th 1824 aged 77 years"

47. Extract from Weymouth's Bury Street Burial Ground gravestone removal register.

A project by Atlantic Geometrics and funded by Historic England and the National Lottery Heritage Fund is under way involving photographing every headstone in Church of England churchyards and cemeteries. The project is estimated to be finished in 2028. This is being carried out on a county by county basis, beginning with Cumbria. Results will show every memorial as well as plotting its location on a graveyard map, which is particularly handy if you wish to visit the plot yourself. The company are using surviving burial records, meaning the location of your ancestor's burial place may be revealed via this research even if they have no surviving headstone. There is no word yet as to when Dorset's data will be available so keep an eye out on their website www.atlanticgeomatics.co.uk/burial-ground-management-system.

Values of the Record

The main value of viewing a memorial inscription is the information it contains. This may include a date of birth, date of death, occupation, relationships and more rarely a cause of death. A biblical verse may be included or any information relating to the person's lifetime achievements if they were of note. Some headstones mention deaths of stillborn children who do not feature in records of burial or baptism. Inscriptions can help find an ancestor's death certificate or burial register entry in the parish registers and an age at death can help find a baptism entry or birth certificate. Surveys carried out in the 1800s are of particular value as they recorded wording from headstones that are no longer legible. You may find 'XP' or 'IHS' inscribed on a headstone. XP are the first two letters of the Greek word for Christ, whereas IHS is a contraction of the Greek word for Jesus.

You may discover images carved into your ancestor's headstone and wish to know what they represent. There are many different symbols and images found on gravestones, some of which are unique to the person. However, most were fairly common and are easy to understand their meaning. A skull simply symbolises death, an hourglass denotes mortality and a dove stands for peace or hope. Some symbols may provide an insight into your ancestor's life, such as those depicting tools of their trade or freemason's symbols hinting at their membership. Some scenes have been depicted on headstones, such as biblical scenes, a landscape view or a depiction of an incident, such as a drowning ship which hints at how the deceased met their demise. It is rare to find imagery and symbols on ledgers.

The size of the headstone and amount of inscription can sometimes imply the wealth and status of a person in the community.

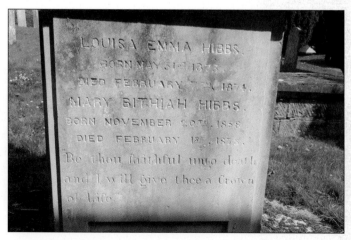

48. *This large tomb in Bere Regis churchyard naming Louisa Emma Hibbs and Mary Bithiah Hibbs implies they came from a wealthy family.*

Limitations of the Record

Many of our ancestors will not have been given a headstone; many shared an unmarked pauper's grave. Even where they were erected, a majority of headstones have not survived. A headstone's survival depends on a range of factors including weathering, the type of stone used and vandalism. There are headstones from the 1600s which are easy to read and others erected in the 1900s which are already badly weathered and therefore illegible.

An ancestor's headstone may not be where you expect it to be. Your ancestor may have moved in later life, perhaps to be cared for by relatives. My great-great grandfather, Walter Eli Hatcher, is buried in Bincombe. His headstone notes his details at the top of a large stone, followed by a large gap and then details of two of his deceased children. The large gap was undoubtedly reserved for his wife Elizabeth so she could also be buried there when her time came. After Walter's death, Elizabeth moved to Broadmayne and as a result she is buried in Broadmayne churchyard.

Unfortunately, many headstones have also been moved within the churchyard. This is usually due to churchyards downsizing. In these cases you will find rows of headstones lined up against the churchyard boundary wall, with many burial plots now built upon.

49. Inscription at Bincombe for Walter Eli Hatcher with a large gap underneath.

The reliability of the information supplied on headstones is questionable. Where possible, the information should always be backed up by other sources. Where a date or year of birth is noted, this may be incorrect by a number of years. People did not keep track of their ages in the same way we do now, so try to be flexible if using this information to find an entry in a baptism register. Some headstones were erected retrospectively meaning even the date of death may have been mis-remembered.

Dorset Examples

In Broadmayne, the memorial stone for my great-grandmother Susan Eunice Hatcher also features her mother (my great-great grandmother) Elizabeth, Susan's second husband Bernard Quinton and their daughter Eileen. All of their full names are given along with the date that they died and their age at the time of their death. The stone featuring four people helps cement the family relationship to the researcher and the stone clearly shows how they are related to each other. Their rough year of birth can be worked out using the figures given on the stone. The earliest death on the stone is that of my second great-grandmother Elizabeth, who died in 1945, however, it is unknown whether the headstone was erected then or at a later date - perhaps after the passing of Susan or Bernard. Where headstones are placed a long time after a person's death, the details provided are more likely to be incorrect. In this case, Elizabeth's age and date of death are correctly given.

My third great-grandparents, Edwin and Mary Hatcher, are buried in Osmington. The memorial inscription on the gravestone gives their names, dates of death, ages at death and their relationship to each other. Under Edwin's details is the quote *For I know that my redeemer liveth* a quotation from the Book of Job in the Old Testament. Underneath Mary's details is the popular phrase *Peace, perfect peace*, from the hymn of the same name. The stone is badly weathered making it hard to read. The details given on the stone are all correct and have been verified with other sources. At the head of the stone is a cross with lines of equal length and rounded ends within a quatrefoil; this is known as a *bottony heraldic cross*, a common Christian symbol.

IN LOVING MEMORY OF
ELIZABETH HATCHER
WHO DIED 30TH JULY 1945
AGED 84 YEARS
ALSO OF HER DAUGHTER
SUSAN EUNICE QUINTON
WHO DIED 27TH NOVEMBER 1983
AGED 86 YEARS
AND THE HUSBAND OF
SUSAN EUNICE
BERNARD PATRICK QUINTON
WHO DIED 11TH MAY 1990
AGED 83 YEARS
AND THEIR DAUGHTER
EILEEN ELIZABETH
GLADWIN
WHO DIED 22ND JANUARY 2010
AGED 71 YEARS

50. Elizabeth's inscription at Broadmayne

51. *Edwin and Mary Hatcher's headstone at Osmington churchyard on the far right. John and Elizabeth Hatcher's headstone is next to it.*

To the left of Edwin and Mary's headstone is that of Edwin's parents. It is common to find graves of relations situated near to each other and it is always worth looking around the area of an ancestor's grave to see if there are any more family headstones nearby. This inscription for my fourth great-grandparents, John and Elizabeth Hatcher, has more damage and is much harder to read. The inscription gives the name of John Hatcher and names Elizabeth as his wife who shares the burial plot. His date of death and age is legible, but unfortunately Elizabeth's is not. No further details are clear and the stone is partially sunk and leaning at an angle.

Many years ago I contacted Osmington church regarding their burials and they sent me a detailed document listing all the monumental inscriptions within the churchyard which had been recorded by Somerset and Dorset Family History Society in 1991. This document was able to fill in the gaps of John and Elizabeth's inscription, including Elizabeth's death date and age. Whilst care should always be taken with the transcriptions by others, there is often no other source that can provide the information. Fortunately, as Elizabeth died in 1875, her date of death and age at death were verified using her death certificate. Pre-civil registration in 1837, there are limited sources to corroborate a date of death, such as burial registers sometimes recording the death date or perhaps a will or deed. These earlier transcriptions can prove invaluable where an inscription is now unreadable and information should always be sought to discover if earlier recordings of the inscriptions have been made.

CHAPTER 13
Tax Lists and Oaths Rolls

About the Record

Tax lists certainly don't sound like the most appealing documents to read but they can provide us with a great deal of information. Genealogists often refer to them as census substitutes, although it is usually only the main householder who is listed. As well as locating our ancestors, the lists can also tell us more about their lives such as how many hearths and windows were in their residence, how much land they owned and they can also hint at a person's financial status. Registers of those who have taken oaths are similar to tax lists - both often comprise a listing of particular people, usually a male head of a household. The records are not always the easiest to locate and survival of the earlier tax lists is fairly low, but they may provide you with a key piece of information that helps you to break down that brick wall you've been working on.

Land tax assessments between 1692 and 1932 were based on a valuation of a person's land. They list the owner of the land, with occupiers named after 1772 and tend to survive best from 1780 onwards. These assessments were used as proof of being eligible to vote. The Marriage Duty Act was a highly unpopular annual tax waged between 1695 and 1705; it was paid by childless widowers, unmarried men aged twenty-five and over, as well as there being an additional tax paid on births, marriages and burials. This ensured almost everyone had to pay the tax, introduced by William III to fund the ongoing war with France. Parish incumbents made lists of those residing in their parish in an attempt not to miss a relevant payment. Where these survive they can act as a mini census for the area.

The hearth tax was introduced in 1662 to provide income for the newly restored monarch, Charles II. Payment was due twice a year and the amount due was dependent on the number of fireplaces and stoves in a property; the tax lasted till 1689. The hearth tax lists give the name of the property occupier in each parish, and the number of hearths in their property. This tax was seen as rather invasive, with assessors sometimes demanding to enter a property to check the occupiers were not lying about how many hearths they had. For this reason, hearth tax was replaced with a window tax, which could be checked from outside the property. Window tax lasted from 1696 -1851. Even today you can see older properties where windows have been blocked up, all in the cause of paying less window tax!

The oldest surviving tax lists in Dorset are the subsidy rolls which go back to 1327. These lay subsidies were introduced in the twelfth century and each payment was based upon the value of an individual's 'moveable goods'. Poll tax began in 1377 and this controversially taxed a wider range of people, including married women, servants and those born abroad.

Oaths similarly give lists of names at varying periods throughout history. The Protestation Oath returns of 1641/2 should name every adult male who declared their loyalty to the Protestant faith, usually compiled by the parish incumbent. The aim of this oath was to reveal who was a Roman Catholic, at a time when attitudes towards the religion were unfavourable. Many Dorset parishes list the recusants who refused to sign at the end of each parish listing. The Association Oath Rolls date from 1696 and were an oath of loyalty to the Crown, the records of which are divided by county.

Sacrament certificates were issued to people wishing to hold public or military office or other official positions of trust after receiving the Sacrament of the Lord's Supper. The certificates were issued to prove that these people were not Catholics; this was a way too of ensuring that no nonconformists held office in the country. The certificates provide the date and place of the communion and were signed by the minister, churchwarden and two witnesses. The office position the person holds is also often provided. Sacrament certificates were also issued to foreign Protestants who wished to live in England after they had also taken the Anglican Communion - most notably the Huguenots who arrived from France.

Locating the Records

Some tax lists and oath rolls have been transcribed and are available free online at Dorset OPC (www.opcdorset.org). The availability for each parish varies, so it is advisable to visit the parish page of interest to see what is available.

Land tax assessments are held by The National Archives in IR 23 for 1798-1914, with those for Dorset in IR 23/21 and IR 23/22. A large collection is also held at Dorset History Centre, available at Ancestry in their 'Dorset, England, Land Tax Returns, 1780 -1832' holding. Very few records relating to the Marriage Duty Act 1695 -1705 survive, aside from the parish registers. There is, however, an excellent set of listings for Lyme Regis. These were researched and published by Dr Judith Ford in 2011 and can be ordered via the Dorset Record Society.

Names of Proprietors.	Names of Occupiers.	Names or Description of Estates or Property.	Sums Assessed and Exonerated.			Sums Assessed and not Exonerated.		
			£	s	D	£	s	D
Mr Edwards	Saml. Granger	Feaver's	"	"	"	"	5	3
Mr Stone	James Arnold	Coombs	"	"	"	"	5	3
Wm Cosens	The Revd. W.H. Trim	Stakeford	"	"	"	"	2	7½
Mr George Bartlett	Himself	Coombs	"	"	"	"	3	11½

52. *Extract of land tax record for Yetminster 1831.*

Hearth tax assessments do not have a great survival rate and the Dorset ones are sadly rather minimal. The best run is for 1662 -1664 and these have been transcribed and published by Cecil Meekings, with a copy held by Dorset History Centre. Some extracts have been transcribed and are available at Dorset OPC, such as those for East Orchard and Up Cerne. Dorset History Centre has a very small collection of hearth tax assessments, such as those for Hinton St Mary in 1664. A majority are held by the National Archives in E 179, with most Dorset records ending before 1675. Dorset History Centre holds the surviving window tax records for the county. The best run is for Lyme Regis dating 1702-1745, with others being more sporadic such as assessments for Edmondsham for 1760 and Horton for 1795.

Many of the Dorset lay subsidy rolls have been published. *The Dorset Lay Subsidy Rolls of 1327* was published by Alexander R Rumble in 1908 and is the earliest surviving tax list for Dorset. In 1971, Anthony David Mills published *The Dorset Lay Subsidy Roll of 1332*. These are out of print, as are other publications relating to Dorset lay subsidies, but used books can be found on online auction sites and in second-hand book shops; these publications can be viewed at Dorset History Centre and some libraries. Most of the original records are held at the National Archives, in series E 179, with a small selection at Dorset History Centre, such as that for Wareham dating 1488 -1489. Some lay subsidies have been transcribed and are available at Dorset OPC, such as for Fontmell Magna. Poll tax records are also held in E 179 at the National Archives. There are many other miscellaneous tax lists, with taxes introduced ranging from employing male and female servants to using wig powder! These are spread between the National Archives and Dorset History Centre and can be located via Discovery by searching for 'tax' and your parish of choice.

The Protestation Returns of 1641/2 are held by the Parliamentary Archives in London and not all survive, with notable omissions being Dorchester, Bridport and Lyme Regis. Many have suffered damage and therefore partial loss including West Knighton, Broadmayne, Wyke Regis and Melcombe Regis. Some transcripts are available for a good number of parishes at Dorset OPC, including Winterborne Clenston, East Stoke and Marnhull. A full transcription of the surviving Protestation Returns for Dorset have been published by Edward Alexander Fry and is available to purchase. Some transcripts are available at Dorset OPC, including Winterborne Clenston, East Stoke and Marnhull. The Association Oath Rolls of 1696 are held at the National Archives in Series C 213. Those for Dorset that survive cover Bere Regis, Bridport, Corfe Castle, Dorchester, Lyme Regis, Poole, Shaftesbury, Wareham and Weymouth.

Dorset History Centre holds many sacrament certificates dating from the seventeenth to nineteenth centuries. A majority of these are catalogued by name of the person taking the oath and so will be found by a simple name search. The names of the minister, churchwarden and witnesses are not given. The Quarter Sessions records held here also name those who took the sacrament, as it was necessary for people to present their certificate to the officials and take an oath in their presence. There are a few Dorset sacrament certificates in other county archives which can be found via The National Archives Discovery catalogue.

Values of the Record

The best thing about of both tax lists and oath rolls is that you can locate a particular person, usually the head of the household, in a named parish. Hearth tax assessments are an excellent example of this. Finding a person's name in the list can help you to discover where they were residing at a certain date, whether they were alive at that time and can lead you to finding them in other records. The names of the householders who were exempt may also be listed; exemption was usually due to poverty. Oath lists tend to cover a larger proportion of a parish than tax registers. Sometimes tax lists and oath registers may use the suffixes of Junior and Senior (written as Jr and Sr). This can be helpful if you have a father and son of the same name living within the same parish as it helps place both of them.

Financial status is hinted at in many of the tax records. Knowing how many hearths or stoves a person had can hint at their prosperity; if they had a large number it may suggest that they were innkeepers or wealthy. If your ancestor paid land tax and is listed as the owner, the amount paid can suggest their wealth according to the amount of land that they owned. Knowing how many windows your ancestor had in their property from the window tax records can indicate the size of their house and therefore suggest their wealth and status too.

Where a good run of unbroken records survive, these can help you to learn when your ancestor moved in and out of a particular parish. When they disappear, this implies that they either moved or died or were exempt, perhaps through poverty. Land tax records are particularly useful for this and you can also track how their tax payment may have changed.

Poll tax records name people who do not often feature in other documents, such as wives and servants, and include a greater percentage of the population than lay subsidies. It may be impossible for you to trace your family back to the earliest tax record of the lay subsidy rolls of 1327, but they can be interesting to view for surname studies. Early records such as these can help us to understand how families moved around the county and further afield and tracking a particular name can also help to understand its origins.

Limitations of the Record

Only a minority of people feature in tax and oath lists and you will usually be looking for the head of a household to appear. If you cannot find your ancestor in one record, try searching in another. For example, they will not appear in land tax records if they did not own or occupy land but they may appear in hearth tax records if they rented a property.

Identification can often prove difficult particularly if your ancestor had a common name, as little other information is usually supplied in tax listings. If there are six John Smiths living within two neighbouring parishes, then it is probably not possible to decipher who is the relevant John to you from tax listings alone. The records can help you to narrow down which parishes he may have been living in and therefore push you to search for other sources from these parishes, which may then help to locate him.

There are a number of exemptions for tax payments. The poor were exempt from paying hearth tax, window tax, lay subsidies and taxes relating to the Marriage Duty Act of 1695. Land tax assessments will only feature land owners, with occupiers from 1772. Certain occupations were also exempt from certain taxes, such as the clergy being excused from paying lay subsidies. If you know your ancestor was living within a parish but they do not feature in a particular tax listing, look at the reasons for exemption and this may explain why they are not on the list. As well as those who were exempt, many others evaded payment.

Oaths also do not cover every member of the population. In some areas the Association Oath Rolls were only signed by gentry and army officers, whereas other parishes record all males aged eighteen and over. Females appear much less frequently in these rolls, as well as the Protestation Oath returns and those aged under eighteen tend not to feature at all. Many of the tax lists do not survive or are very damaged, particularly the earlier records such as lay subsidy rolls and poll tax lists. In the Dorset Protestation Oath Returns, some parishes name their recusants clearly and some state the parish had no recusants, whereas other parishes do not state either. This makes it difficult to work out how many men are missing from the returns. Some parishes stated that several of their men were 'at sea', with some of these men named in their absence but usually not.

Dorset Examples

My fifth great-grandfather, Thomas Osment, can be seen in the land tax returns for 1792, 1793 and 1794 as an occupier of a property in Sutton Poyntz. Thomas paid 2s 3¾d tax quarterly, with the owner of the house named as William Doe, his father-in-law and my sixth great-grandfather. These returns are available as part of the 'Dorset, England, Land Tax Returns, 1780-1832' collection on Ancestry. Thomas died in 1794. After this date the land tax returns lists William Doe as the owner and occupier of the same property, having moved in after Thomas' death. The relationship is not stated on the tax returns itself and is only found through other sources; however, this proves that it is always worth making a note of who owned the property occupied by your ancestor, in case they are related.

53. Extract from the 1794 land tax record showing Thomas Osment occupying a house owned by William Doe in Sutton Poyntz.

The 1641/2 Protestation Oath Returns feature my eleventh great-grandfathers, Peter Gover and Henry Tarry. They are both seen in Swanage, having taken the oath on the 20 Feb 1641/2. There are three other Govers in the parish - Emanuel, William and John, and two other Tarrys - Samuel and John. These names provide leads as to potential relatives, but the oaths cannot be used for this purpose alone.

Looking at the hearth tax list for Swanage for 1664, only Samuel Tarry appears and there are no Govers named. My ancestor Peter Gover died in Swanage in 1665 so his absence from the list could mean he was in another parish, evaded the tax or may no longer have been the head of the household. No burial or year of death has been found yet for Henry Tarry, so his absence from the hearth tax list may indicate his decease.

Looking at the lay subsidy rolls for Dorset in 1332, it is important to bear in mind that surnames were not necessarily hereditary at this time. There is evidence that by 1350, a majority of people in the south had begun to use hereditary surnames. At the time this tax listing was taken, it is possible that some people will have surnames that were completely different from their parents and from their children. Whilst this record is therefore difficult to use from a genealogical point of view for this reason, let alone the (usually) impossible task of researching a tree branch back this far, there is definite interest in viewing the roll.

There are many parishes featuring people of the same surname in the 1332 rolls, such as De Agnete Niwman and De Johanne Niwman, residing in Winterborne Stickland, and De Rogero Ker and De Nicholao Ker residing in Winterborne Clenston. Another interesting example is that of De Henrico *atte* Brygge and De Willelmo *atte* Brygge, both living in Osmington. The surname of '*atte* Brygge' translates into *at the bridge*, given to those living at or near a bridge within the parish. Therefore, Henrico and Willelmo (who today would be known as Henry and William) may be unrelated and have been given the same surname due to where they lived. Or it is possible that they were brothers and their father was the one originally given the surname due to his location and the name was then passed on. See the chapter on surnames in this book for more information.

CHAPTER 14
Title Deeds

About the Record

For years I avoided using title deeds as part of my research. I found the idea of them daunting and so didn't even attempt to use them for a long time. I fear this is the case for many family historians who, like myself in the past, don't understand their value or are put off by their legal jargon. Honestly, title deeds take a bit of practice to get used to but I hope that by reading this chapter you will feel encouraged to give them a try. They can contain unique scraps of information that won't be found elsewhere and may help you break down your brick wall. Title deeds are used by house historians to trace property ownership but these interesting documents can equally be used by genealogists.

A title deed was created to transfer property from one person to another in a legally binding document. Property may be freehold, leasehold or copyhold. The information below states the different types of property ownership and the terms attached to these.

Freehold - Fee Simple - Property ownership could be passed onto anybody by purchasing it, gifting it or bequeathing it without restriction.

Freehold - Fee Tail - Property ownership was limited to transfer only to descendants of the original estate owner. The land could not be sold or bequeathed but the deed kept the property within the same family.

Freehold - Life Estate - Property held by a person for the rest of their life. The tenant can lease or mortgage the property. Upon the tenant's death, the property reverts to the original property owner.

Leasehold - Property held by a lease which was held for a specified amount of time. Payment could be in a lump sum or in the form of regular rent payments to the land owner.

Copyhold - Property owned by copy of a court roll, such as from a manor court. The tenants needed the permission of the lord of the manor to transfer, mortgage or sub-let their land.

There are many different types of historical title deeds and these can be helpful albeit a bit tricky to understand. The most common title deeds you are likely to come across are below:

Final Concord (Fine) - The record of a fictitious court case where the querent (plaintiff) demanded property from the deforciant (vendor). The property value stated was often incorrect.

Common Recovery - Another fictitious dispute heard in court to transfer property ownership and have proof in writing.

Bargain and Sale - An early form of conveyance where the purchaser paid a set sum of money to the vendor for property ownership.

Lease and Release - Property was conveyed by two documents. The first is the lease. The next day the release would be recorded, stating the vendor relinquished his ownership of the property to the person he leased it to the previous day for the sum of the property's value.

Don't feel that you have to memorise and learn the information above. If you wish, you may find it easier to refer back to this information once you have found a title deed relevant to your family. You may never come across some types of deed, so don't worry if you don't understand any of the information; it may never become relevant to your family history research anyway!

The National Land Registry was established in 1862 on a voluntary basis. From 1899 onwards, it became compulsory for more and more different types of land and property to be registered so you are more likely to find a relevant entry for your ancestors land from this date. For most properties you can download a copy of the title plan and title register for a small fee. I recently downloaded a title plan for just £3.

Locating the Record

A majority of surviving historical title deeds are held at the National Archives and local archives. Regarding local archives or Dorset, most are held at Dorset History Centre, but there is no requirement for deeds to be held in the county in which the property was located thus, they are held all over the country. For example, deeds relating to Dorset can be found at Devon Archives, West Sussex Record Office and Isle of Wight Record Office. In most cases these deeds relate to larger estates so unless your family are of noble heritage, they are more than likely to be found in Dorset History Centre. They hold thousands of title deeds. If a search here is fruitless, consider branching out. Certain types of deed are held by the National Archives. Final Concords are held at CP25, with Common Recoveries are at CP40 and CP43. TNA also holds a wide range of other title deeds that have been deposited there however many have not yet been indexed.

The best way to search for title deeds for a particular person or parish is to search via the National Archives Discover catalogue online. By using one search term such as 'Stourpaine Title Deeds' or 'Blundell Title Deeds', you can find the catalogued entries for all title deeds relating to Stourpaine parish or the Blundell surname across all archives in the country. Depending on how many results there are, you can filter these accordingly, such as adding your ancestor's first name or narrowing the search to Dorset History Centre only if you wish. This is not foolproof and depends on how each item is catalogued. Some do not feature 'title deed' in their title or description and appear under the type of deed such as 'lease and release'. Where deeds have been indexed the names are usually mentioned unless they are illegible.

Some of the catalogue entries for local archives are excellent, effectively transcribing the most useful information from the document. Dorset History Centre is excellent for this. These can tell you the type of deed, its date and the names of the parties involved. There are many examples where family members are also named within the catalogue, together with their relationship. In these cases, ensure you still view the original document so no detail is missed and use the transcription as a guide to help you. Unfortunately many deeds are still not catalogued.

Some title deeds remain in private hands. This may be the case where the deeds relate to a particular estate that has chosen to retain them. Title deeds are also sometimes sold in charity shops and online auctions, meaning they can end up anywhere in the world and be untraceable. If you cannot find a title deed relating to a relevant ancestor, in a majority of cases it will have been destroyed.

Copies of title plans and the title register can be downloaded from the HM Land Registry's official website at https://www.gov.uk/government/organisations/land-registry.

Values of the Record

Title deeds can tell us whether the property in question was freehold, leasehold or copyhold, giving an insight into our ancestor's property ownership terms. The value of the property they owned is usually stated, although this is sometimes fictional. Depending on the type of deed, other information may also be given. Deeds were sometimes part of a bond, marriage settlement or mortgage, all of which can provide extra genealogical information. Where a property was inherited rather than purchased, it is possible that a copy of the relevant will may be found amongst the deeds. You may also find copies of birth, marriage and death certificates filed with the deed, or even extracts from parish registers. These are particularly useful if the parish register itself has not survived.

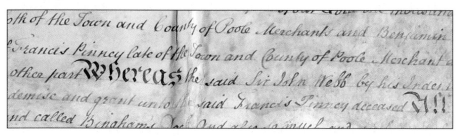

54. Title deed extract dated 1795 naming Francis Pinney, deceased merchant of Poole.

The most obvious values of a title deed are the names of the property owners, their occupations and residences. This is the basic information that is usually supplied from a genealogical standpoint. Depending on the type of property ownership and deed, more information may be given. Three-life leases are useful as these name three people who would own the property, one after the other. This was often a man, his wife and their child. Their names and sometimes ages are given. Copyhold for lives was a similar scenario where the property belonged to a number of named people, again usually three. Where more than one person is named in a deed, their relationship is often stated.

Prior to 1925, it was essential for property and landowners to keep all the relevant title deeds relating to their house and land regardless of date. This means they are often found in bundles in archives where a large bundle will contain all of the deeds relating to one specific property. You may strike it lucky and find a bundle of deeds relating to your family tree where a property has remained in the family for generations. Even if only one of the deeds is relevant to your ancestors, it can be of interest to view the deeds before and after that to see how the ownership changed and if there were any changes to the property during your ancestor's time there and any changes in value. The deed after your ancestor owned the property can sometimes give the death date of the former owner, so it's worth a check if you do find a bundle.

You may find it interesting to read about the description of the property and land in question. These may sometimes be vague referring to tenements and outbuildings without much detail but there is usually something of interest. The fields belonging to your ancestor may be named; these may then be located on a map, such as an enclosure map. The size of the property may be stated and the location within the parish is also generally given. Unfortunately due to the dates of the document, this is rarely as simple as reading 30 Smith Avenue as this will likely be a time before properties were numbered and roads were named. Instead they will be located by features in the landscape. Perhaps your ancestor owned land near a woodland or lake? Neighbours are often named in deeds which can also be of interest.

Limitations of the Record

Title deeds can admittedly be laborious documents to deal with, often comprising large pieces of paper full of legal jargon in writing that is hard to read. Initially it can take time and practice to understand which parts of the document will be of interest to you as a family historian; it can be easy to scan over the document quickly and miss a key piece of information. The large deeds often have little punctuation as we know it today. Try not to feel overwhelmed by a title deed and take your time with each record. They are *not* impossible to understand so break each line down, one by one, and transcribe the words that you can read easily. This will help you to recognise commonly used phrases.

Some title deeds were written in Latin until 1733, such as Final Concords. This can seem off-putting at first but it is just another challenge to overcome. The first step is to learn what your ancestor's name is in Latin; Johannes for John, for example. You can then scan a document for their name and begin to translate the sentences in which their name appears. There is rarely a need to transcribe the entire document. You could choose to hire someone to translate the document for you to ensure you don't miss any information. If you have found a document in Latin relating to an ancestor, remember that this could hold a unique detail that you won't find elsewhere, so it is best not to ignore it.

Many title deeds have been lost. After the Law of Property Act of 1925, only title deeds relating to the previous thirty years had to be kept meaning many were subsequently destroyed at this time. People simply didn't want to keep documents that they no longer needed. Some are still held in private hands. Those that are held

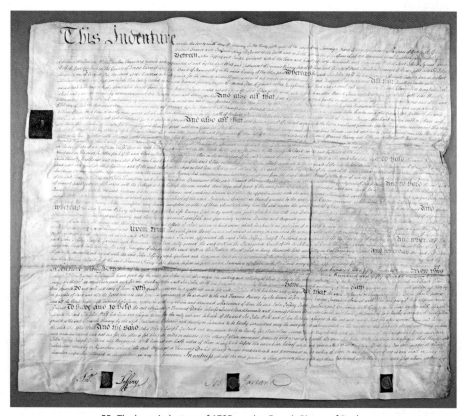

55. *The large indenture of 1795 naming Francis Pinney of Poole.*

110

by archives are often not indexed, meaning that searching for your ancestor by name will not bring up the relevant result. Instead, they are often catalogued under vague headings such as 'Miscellaneous title deeds', meaning they are almost impossible to find. Gradually archives are improving this system and more names are being added.

Dorset Examples

A lease dating 27 Apr 1686 refers to my tenth great-grandfather, Samuel Tarry, who leased a dwelling house and arable fields in Swanage from Lewis Corham. None of Samuel's family members are named, but there are snippets of interesting information in the deed. The location of the property is well detailed - *the land of Thomas Corham on the east, a small lane or drove on the west, the street highway on the north and the land of the rectory of Sandwhich on the South.*

56. *The 1686 title deed surrounding Samuel Tarry's lease in Swanage. Note the wavy lines at the top of the document, a key feature of an indenture.*

His yearly rent was one half-penny which was *due on the Feast Day of St. Michael the Archangel*, otherwise known as Michaelmas (29 Sep). Samuel's occupation is given as a marbler, an occupation he shared with his son James.

A different example features several of my ancestors in one document. This deed is related to another lease which is more complex naming multiple parties and is a much larger document. The lease dates from 29 Jan 1795 and therefore uses more recognisable language than the earlier deed of Samuel Tarry. This document is about land that was leased by my eighth great-grandfather Francis Pinney of Poole from Sir John Webb. The deed nicely ties up with facts known from other sources. For example, Francis is stated to have been deceased and from burial records I am aware he died in 1790. His occupation is given as a merchant and that matches his will and an early newspaper record. The date of his will is also given in the deed, as well as stating it was proved at Prerogative Court of Canterbury.

New information gained from the deed includes the description of the land he was leasing and the fact that Francis commissioned the building of Bingham Docks in Hamworthy. The location of this is clearly stated in a similar manner to Samuel's leased land. The lease names Francis' nephew, Richard Pinney, and his two grandsons Isaac and John Frampton, the latter being my sixth great-grandfather. The lease names a previous lease holder called John Carter, as well as his son William, daughter Rebecca and her husband James Seager. It is not uncommon to find such a wealth of genealogical information in one deed and so they are always worth searching for. A simple name search on Dorset History Centre's catalogue is the best place to start.

CHAPTER 15
Manorial Records

About the Record

Manors were territorial and administrative divisions based on the old feudal system of land tenancy. Manor boundaries did not always share the same border as parishes - there may be more than one manor within a parish or more than one parish within a manor. The documents that we term as 'manorial records' consist of manorial court rolls, accounts, presentments, surveys and maps and for Dorset they survive from the fourteenth century.

Manorial records are some of the most underused sources available to genealogists and it is easy to see why – they can seem daunting, overwhelming and vastly complicated, a bit like Title Deeds. But, fear not, as they are much easier to find now thanks to the National Archives database.

Some manorial records are difficult to read and understand – the text is very small and generally abbreviated. Many early manorial records are written in Latin which is a bit of a step for most of us and even when translated the text can be hard to interpret. But they are extremely useful to genealogists as they have so much information in them. They also help us learn more about our ancestors' characters and run-ins with the manorial courts.

There were two types of manorial court - the Court Baron and the Court Leet. From a genealogical perspective, the Court Baron is the most useful as this is more likely to mention names of different generations of the same family. This court was held once every three weeks and dealt with land transfer and management. The Court Leet was held usually every six months and dealt with minor crime committed within the manor. The Court Leets of the Manor of Wareham and The Island & Royal Manor of Portland still exist today, taking on a rather different format. The minutes of both the Court Baron and the Court Leet were written into court rolls which is what we peruse today. If your ancestor was an official within the manor, such as a constable, reeve or steward, or if they were on the court jury, then they will be named regularly as being in attendance in court or for notification of their appointment. Those who were excused from attending are also usually named. The jury consisted of manorial tenants and were known as the 'homage'.

Presentments are the notes made by the steward prior to writing them into the court rolls. This means they are an excellent substitute for missing court rolls but are also interesting in their own right, including the marks and signatures of court witnesses. There is a good collection for Dorset, although not for every parish.

Manorial surveys are unique and were created for a specific purpose, for example if a new lord of the manor wanted to assess the total value of his land. Some are very detailed, naming fields and plotting their boundaries, naming tenants and the rent that they paid along with a map highlighting each property. These maps of the manor may be the earliest map for the area. The income produced from various plots may also be given. A majority do not have maps attached and many surveys are rather vague.

57. *Extract from a survey for Sutton Poyntz Manor detailing the land held by Josias Croad and George Thorn in 1832.*

There are four types of manorial surveys; rentals, extents, terriers and custumals. Rent rolls, more commonly known as rentals, survive from the seventeenth century and are lists of tenants with the rent that they owed. Extents list the rent of every building and plot of land in the manor. Terriers and custumals are seen less frequently. Custumals record the tenants of the manor, their holdings and obligations whilst terriers were written geographical descriptions of the manor, sometimes naming field owners. For Dorset there are 411 rentals, forty-seven extents, twenty-six custumals and twenty-nine terriers known to exist.

Locating the Record

The best place to begin your search for a manorial record is the Manorial Documents Register available on the National Archives website at https:// discovery.nationalarchives.gov.uk/manor-search. This is a free and easy-to-use service which lists the documents that have survived for each manor and within which archive or repository you can find them. Some manorial documents remain in private hands and are not listed. On the website, the easiest way to search is via the pre-selected 'Search by Manor' option, select the historic county of 'Dorset' (or other if the boundaries have changed or you are searching elsewhere) and type in

Description	Held by	Reference
1394-1394: valor, with other manors (French)	Devon Archives and Local Studies Service (South West Heritage Trust)	CR/531
1514-1514: reeve's account, with other manors	Devon Archives and Local Studies Service (South West Heritage Trust)	CR/528
1526-1527: account, with other manors	The National Archives	SC 6/Hen VIII/6174

58. A snippet from Ibberton Manor's entry in the Manorial Documents Register.

the name of the parish you are interested in. The results may be focused on one manor, or several manors, depending upon how many manors relate to that parish.

Typing in the parish name of Ibberton gives one simple result of 'Ibberton Manor' which has eight manorial records held at three different archives. These are all clearly listed noting the type of record, the years it relates to, the archive where it is held and its reference number at the archive. For example, a rental dating 1810 -1816 is held at Dorset History Centre under the reference D/PIT/M79. This reference can then be used at Dorset History Centre to access the record of interest. Melbury Osmond has thirty-eight manorial records held at four separate archives - Dorset History Centre, The National Archives, Wiltshire and Swindon History Centre and Kresen Kernow. These are again all clearly listed in the same manner and in date order.

Other parishes will have multiple results if there is more than one manor within a parish. Bere Regis parish consisted of Bere Regis Manor and Shitterton Manor. In some cases it is easy to work out in which manor your ancestor's property would have been; in cases such as Shitterton it's easier as it has clear boundaries. In other cases it may appear confusing, but a surviving manorial map should help.

Values of the Record
Manorial court rolls can provide much value to family historians. Finding your ancestor named in a roll can help to locate him or her in a certain area and guide you where to research next, for example in parish registers. The parish of residence of officials is normally stated on their appointment. If a person was punished for a minor act such as not controlling their livestock or perhaps using false weights to sell goods, this can give you details as to their occupation and sometimes name relationships are given too. If they were a repeat offender this can give an insight into their character. Why were they pronounced guilty and of what crime? Were they defiant in changing their ways? Common crimes were assault and poaching

with anything more serious being referred to the Assizes court. Chances are if your ancestor features in the court rolls accused of an offence, it is likely very minor such as neglecting their care of weeds or blocking a drain.

The Court Baron recording copyhold land transfers is arguably of the greatest use to researchers. Both the old and new tenant were often related and their names and relationship will be given - for example a son inheriting land upon the death of his father. There may be extracts from other relevant historical documents, such as wills which relate to the property transfer. Copyhold tenants required permission from the Court Baron if they wanted to inherit, buy, sell or mortgage their property and details surrounding this can be found in court rolls. When a copyhold tenant died, a description of his land is given as well as the terms of his tenancy agreement and sometimes details of his death, such as the place and date.

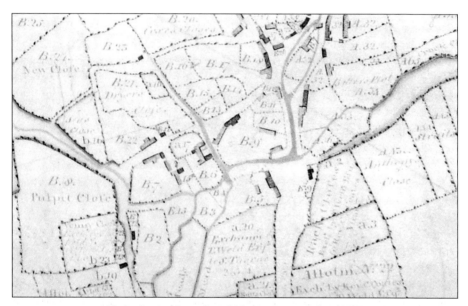

59. A snippet of Sutton Poyntz Manor survey map dated 1796.

The most detailed manorial surveys and maps can help you plot where your ancestors lived, the extent of their property, the rent they paid and their actual residence within the manor. Rentals can sometimes be used to track when an ancestor moved in and out of a manor boundary. Unfortunately there is not often a clear run of several years of rentals to be able to do this in practice.

Limitations of the Record
The least used manorial records are the accounts; this is because they are largely of limited use. They will name tenants for being fined or paying rent and payments

to named tradesman such as carpenters and masons, but its genealogical use is fairly limited and it is highly unlikely any relationships will be stated here. However, they can give an interesting insight into manorial life.

Manorial maps created by a hired surveyor were accurate and detailed, but some were created by the steward as a rough outline for the lord as to the value of property and approximate sizes of pieces of land. They are generally not to scale and so their reliability is questionable. So long as the survey met its purpose and the steward and the lord could interpret it, they weren't too worried about the details and scale being exact.

Manorial records are kept in various archives across England. For example, Marnhull Manor has records at Dorset History Centre, Gloucestershire Archives, Wiltshire and Swindon History Centre, Longleat House and the British Library. If you are interested in one specific record, then it is easy to see where it is held, but depending on how many records you are interested in viewing and where they are held, this can make it an expensive research task. Whether you choose to visit the archives in person or pay for the research to be done for you, the cost can soon add up. It is always worth checking the relevant archives catalogue for the particular record as sometimes, with the older manorial records, they are not fit to be given out for research. This could save you a long trip for no reason!

The biggest limitation is the number of records that have been lost and many just do not survive. Pimperne Manor only has surviving records from 1328 -1548 whilst Leigh Manor only has two records surviving dating 1735 -1748. It is very common to find large gaps in the records where nothing is listed, such as Blandford Forum Manor which has a good collection of court rolls for 1390 - 1392 and 1501 - 1564 but a noticeable gap between 1393 and 1500.

Dorset Examples

The Manorial Documents Register helpfully shows the surviving manorial documentation for each manor, including my choice of Sutton Poyntz Manor. The National Archives holds manor court rolls for the area dating 1450 -1452, with all other surviving rolls at Dorset History Centre. These surviving rolls date 1465 - 1506, 1524 -1542, 1601-1655, 1808 -1865 and 1867-1909. There are clear gaps, particularly for the eighteenth century where none survive. Looking at a court entry dated 30 Oct 1834 (D-WLC/M/104), it notes Joseph Weld Esq was Lord of the Manor and John Barlow was his steward. The officers of the manor are then named, including John Waters as the Bailiff and George Hooper as the Hayward. The Jury and Homage are then listed, featuring twelve men including Robert Squibb, my first cousin six times removed. Robert is one of only two illiterate men in attendance, signing with his mark (a cross) rather than his name.

A later manor court entry dating 22 Oct 1867 (D-WLC/M/110) names Joseph

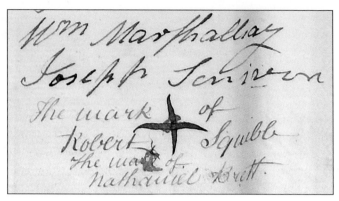

60. *Extract of the signatures and marks of the homage*
of Sutton Poyntz Manor 1834.

Weld Esq again as the Lord of the Manor and Richard Nicholas Howard of Weymouth as his Steward. It is noted that he replaced Charles Bartlett who died that year. This shows how even the simplest of court rolls can help us to track down our ancestors within a particular place, learn their occupation or standing as an official in the manor, discover their literacy ability and find dates of death for officials.

There are four manorial surveys which survive for Sutton Poyntz, all of which are held at Dorset History Centre. They date 1640, 1654, 1832 and 1865, with a gap again for the eighteenth century. The 1832 survey is very useful to genealogists, listing all householders living within the manor, a description of the property, the names of the lives the property is held under and the amount of rent paid. My fifth great-grandfather John Read is listed as renting a cottage and garden for one shilling, with his son Thomas named under Lives. My fourth great-uncle, Josias Croad, is also named as renting a meadow called Cox's Mead for five pounds. Where children are named in the 'Lives' column, their ages are usually given, such as nine-year-old Joseph Tasker. You can therefore use this survey to discover a person's property details, relationships, ages and rent paid, indicating their financial status.

If you still feel a bit daunted at the prospect of using manorial records, I recommend using some from the nineteenth century first to get used to the layout and language used. You will also likely be used to the style of writing from the time from other historic documents you have already looked at. Alternatively you could get hold of a copy of a recent book by Ian Waller – *Introducing Manorial Records*. Published in 2020, this book will answer all your questions about manorial records.

CHAPTER 16

Miscellaneous Sources

Poll Books and Electoral Rolls

Poll books 1696 -1868 are annual listings naming those who were entitled to vote and showing how they voted on which date. Only the wealthiest members of society were qualified to vote, with only three per cent of the population in England and Wales being eligible in 1884. Only men will be found in poll books and many are available to view on Ancestry. My eighth great-grandfather, Francis Pinney, can be seen in a poll book dated 1779. The register states Francis resided in Poole and owned property in Portsea. Francis voted for Whig candidate Jervoise Clark Jervoise who won the election.

Gradually over time, the required voting qualifications were relaxed so that by 1928 all men and women were able to vote. Electoral rolls can be searched from the early twentieth century. Many are available online, such as on Ancestry where the Dorset collection dates 1839 -1922 and contains over one and a half million names. Early rolls are alphabetical by surname, with later rolls from 1918 organised by street for larger parishes, so it would be helpful to know the address at which your ancestors were residing at the time. These rolls show everyone in the household who was qualified to vote, although there are some gaps in the records.

61. Extract from the 1918 electoral register for Bincombe showing the Hatcher family.

My great-great grandfather, Walter Eli Hatcher, features in several electoral registers. He can be seen in the 1918 register residing in Bincombe. Other Hatchers from the same parish include Elizabeth, his wife and Frederick Walter, their son. Both Walter and Frederick are deemed able to vote due to their residence and occupational qualification, with Elizabeth able to vote due to her husband's occupation.

Equity Court Records

The Equity Courts dealt with civil cases using fairness and morality rather than laws; they covered topics such as probate disputes, issues with debts, loan repayments, land disputes and marriage settlements. There were many equity courts where an ancestor may have appeared - the Courts of Chancery, Exchequer, Wards, Requests and Star Chamber. The Court of Chancery largely dealt with land disputes; the Court of Exchequer with financial disputes; the Court of Requests with cases relating to paupers; the Court of Wards with issues surrounding orphans and mentally ill and the Court of Star Chamber with offences against the public order. Despite this, there was a lot of overlap between the courts and it can be a bit unpredictable as to which court your ancestor may have appeared; they were all situated in Westminster, but people travelled from all over the country to appear.

The Court of Chancery was the busiest court and requires a different research technique from the other equity courts, whose records are usually held together. The best way to search for Chancery cases prior to 1876 is to use the National Archives online Discovery catalogue by typing in your ancestor's name and narrowing down the results to search in the 'C' Series only. The title of the cases will usually feature the surnames of the parties involved in the dispute as in *Sugden v Marshall*. To find relevant cases for your family, it is recommended to search for the surname of your ancestor and the parish where they lived.

The catalogued results vary in detail, with some being very brief only naming the plaintiffs, defendants and subject as in *Property in Gillingham*, whereas others provide more information including the residence, occupation and marital status of both the plaintiff and defendants, and the relationship to each other. If your ancestor had a rare surname or lived in a small parish, you can search using just one of these terms in the C Series to see the relevant results. When you have found a case that you believe relates to your family, you can use the reference number to view the documents on site at TNA or to order a copy. From 1876 the cases have not yet been indexed. Try searching newspaper records to discover the title of a case and use this to track the document down at TNA.

Records found from equity court cases include depositions (witness statements), court order books, pleadings, petitions and supporting documents used in the courts. It can be hard to know if you have gathered all of the relevant documents to a particular case, particularly as cases could also move between different courts.

Chancery Cases after 1876 are held in J Series, Exchequer in E Series, Wards in WARD Series, Requests largely in REQ 1-4 and Star Chamber are mostly held in STAC 1-10. All documents remain at the National Archives.

Inquest Records
Inquests were carried out by the local coroner after a person's unexplained or sudden death in order to establish the cause of death. These deaths were often reported in newspapers so where coroners' reports have not survived, the article

may provide extra useful information. Inquest records are not open for public use until they are over seventy-five years old and survival rates are low. Many people come across them in their local archive by chance when they have carried out a simple name search for their ancestor. They were filed with Quarter Sessions records until 1860, many of which are available online at Ancestry. The best surviving records of inquests held at Dorset History Centre cover Poole 1589 -1884, Lyme Regis 1723 -1836, Cogdean Hundred 1804 -1838 and Badbury Hundred 1680 -1842. Inquest records will detail the circumstances of the death, for example if it was due to a fall, if the person had been drinking or if the weather played a part. Details of the person's employment may be given, particularly if the death occurred whilst they were at work. Inquests were also held in cases of suspected suicide. Any surviving witness statements surrounding a suspected suicide can be particularly informative with regards to the deceased's financial, health and personal worries.

The inquest of Thomas Bugden of Christchurch took place on the day he died - 12 Jul 1765 - at Wimborne in the Hundred of Badbury. The coroner was Edward James Baker and there were twelve jurors named who all either signed the document or left their mark. The only personal details of Thomas Bugden that are given are his residence of Christchurch and his occupation as a labourer. No age is stated, nor relatives named. The document is short at just under two small pages of writing. The inquest established that Thomas died whilst digging chalk with John Miller after a load of chalk and earth fell onto him, causing his back and legs to break; the document claimed he died instantly. At a time long before death certificates were issued, this inquest helps to provide the researcher with Thomas' date and cause of death, his residence and occupation possibly helping to prove identification of the right man.

Hospitals and Psychiatric Care
Historically, private medical treatment was available to anyone who could afford it. For those too poor to pay, care could be provided in a workhouse. The National Archives holds the Hospital Records Database at www.nationalarchives.gov.uk/hospitalrecords/default.asp, although this is no longer being updated. This database can be searched to discover more about the history of individual hospitals. For example, searching for Bridport Hospital tells us that it was previously known as Bridport Dispensary and Cottage Hospital and was founded in 1867. Its current address and two previous addresses are given. The database shows where surviving records can be found, which will usually be at Dorset History Centre. Other historic hospitals in Dorset include Lyme Regis Hospital established in 1873 and Weymouth and Dorset County Royal Eye Infirmary established in 1836.

When looking at hospital records, the most useful ones are likely to be the patient records, including admission and discharge registers. These registers can give you the person's name, age, occupation, parish of residence, the date they were admitted and the name of the doctor who was looking after them. If a patient died whilst under their care, their cause of death is usually listed. Many other administrative records survive such as meeting minutes and financial records but these are of limited interest to a genealogist.

Dorset County Hospital originated as a charity in 1840 with only twenty beds in a building in Somerleigh Road in Dorchester town centre. This grew over time to admit an ever-increasing number of patients. A website dedicated to the history of Dorset County Hospital in Dorchester can be viewed at https://historydch.com/. This helpfully shows which records survive and which are open to the public, as well as their archive reference number. There are some free transcripts on their website, including a patient register dating 1851-3 and extracts from the Management Committee Minutes dating 1851-1894.

The in-patient register from Dorset County Hospital shows that twenty-two-year-old Susan Baker of Charminster was admitted in March 1853 and was placed under Dr Cowdell's care. Unfortunately, Susan died of phthisis, another name for tuberculosis. Other causes of death are not so self-explanatory, such as fifteen-year-old Simeon Williams of Bridport admitted in October 1854 and who died because of an 'accident'. If you find your ancestor in a case such as this, try searching for inquest records or newspaper reports of the incident. A majority of patients were cured and these records can add an interesting insight into an affliction suffered by your ancestor that may not be otherwise obvious from other sources. For example, in 1861 fourteen-year-old Eliza Hurst of West Knighton was treated for the skin condition psoriasis, five-year-old Albert Voss of Dorchester was treated for a fractured thigh bone and nineteen-year-old Martha Gill of Wimborne was cured after suffering from sciatica.

Care of the mentally ill has been revolutionised in modern times and it is important to recognize that certain terms, such as 'lunatic' or 'idiot' are thought of differently today. Justices of the Peace used to be responsible for inspecting the three private psychiatric hospitals in the county, known as asylums, at Cranborne, Halstock and Stockland. Records of their inspections survive for 1774 -1858 at Dorset History Centre, with records from 1825 recording inmates' names and details including their age, residence, occupation and the date they were certified to be 'insane'. Dorset History Centre also holds records for the County Asylum at Forston House near Charminster, as well as Herrison House. Records of a sensitive nature are closed for 100 years to protect the confidentiality of those still living.

School Records

Attendance at school was not compulsory until 1880 when children were ordered to attend until the age of ten. You may find records prior to this, with some surviving as far back as the 1500s. These are usually held by county record offices, such as Dorset History Centre, and records include attendance registers, punishment books, minutes of Guardians and log books recording daily events such as exam results, the weather and attendance figures. Admission registers were completed when the child was first admitted to the school and record personal information such as date of birth, address and next of kin. Annotated notes may include reasons for leaving their previous school and if they died during their time in education. If your ancestor was a teacher, the log book can be of particular interest, with teachers often being named including the classes they taught, the dates that they taught at the school and any absences. Most contain detailed daily journal-like entries with some noting what songs were sung that day or what illnesses were ailing the staff or pupils that week; these entries were completed by the head teacher. Log books for Dorset schools survive from 1860 onwards. School records are a fantastic resource, helping us learn more about our ancestors' childhoods for which records are often scarce.

Some school records have been transcribed on opcdorset.org, such as a school log book for Yetminster dated 1877-1883. Transcribed notes here include John Vardy being absent from school with chickenpox on 10 Dec 1877, a school closure on 20 Jan 1881 due to heavy snow and the death of pupil Ernest Lankshear on 11 Jul 1878 with his sister Annie also absent for this reason. It can be fascinating to see what illnesses were spreading through the school at the time, with common entries featuring chickenpox and whooping cough. Teachers are also named, such as Emma Squires who was absent for a week from the 23 Mar 1881 due to her father being seriously ill, leaving Mrs Jeffery to take her place. There are further transcriptions on OPC Dorset of school log books for Longburton, Piddlehinton, Holwell, Lydlinch, Ryme Intrinseca and Sandford Orcas. Check their website for any further additions. You may also find your ancestor's academic achievements noted in the local newspaper.

Divorce

Divorces prior to 1858 were referred to as separations and could be granted by the ecclesiastical courts under very strict rules. This is a rare find. Alternatively, the wealthier classes could obtain a private Act of Parliament to end their marriage. The Court for Divorce and Matrimonial Causes was established in 1858, before being transferred to the Probate, Divorce and Admiralty division in 1873. Divorce was rare until the 1920s and until 1927 all divorce cases were heard in London. A huge majority of divorce documentation from 1938 has been destroyed, but those for 1858 -1937 largely survive and can be accessed at the National Archives. Searching their catalogue for the couple's names should yield a result if the papers survive. Some older documents relating to separation granted by the ecclesiastical court survive at Dorset History Centre, with records of private Acts of Parliament granted pre-1858 held at the Parliamentary Archives.

My great-grandparents Ernest William Taylor and Susan Eunice Hatcher married on 1 Jan 1917 at Bincombe. In November 1917 their only child together, my grandmother Dorothy, was born. Military records show Ernest was a victim of severe shell shock in 1918 and returned to his home county of Kent. Shortly afterwards in April 1919 he married Bertha Langridge in Kent, despite still being married to Susan at the time. The following year in December 1920 Ernest married for a third time - this time to Elsie Oakland in Warwickshire. To find an ancestor married three times within the space of four years without being widowed is quite something! Somehow, Susan found out about Ernest's second marriage to Bertha and in 1924 she filed for divorce. Their final decree is dated 26 Jul 1926.

The records, from the National Archives, show that Ernest failed to turn up at court and could not be traced. The authorities remained unaware of his third marriage. The papers are useful and provide much information which helps our understanding the chain of events and provide the dates of his first two marriages, their location, as well as the addresses at which they were all residing at the time of the marriages. Susan's maiden name is provided, as is Bertha's new married name. The divorce papers name Dorothy as their only child, with Susan winning full custody of her.

> between   Susan Eunice Taylor (then Hatcher spinster)
>
> the Petitioner and   Ernest Taylor
>
>   the Respondent
>
> be dissolved by reason that since the celebration thereof the said Respondent has
>   bigamy with
> been guilty of adultery

62. Snippet *from Susan and Ernest's divorce papers dated 1924.*

Sport

Your ancestor may have been involved in sport professionally or, more likely, as a hobby. Dorset has a rich sporting history, but it is not always obvious as to what sports our ancestors may have played. Cycling clubs were particularly popular in the late 1800s and early 1900s, with a club formed at Poole in 1878 with a membership fee of five shillings; Wimborne's cycling club was established the following year, known as the Wandering Minstrels. Dorset has never had a first class county cricket team but the sport remained popular with amateur teams. Club cricket has been played at a huge number of parishes including Weymouth, Maiden Newton, Blandford Forum and Puddletown. Other notable sporting clubs include football clubs at Portland, Bridport, Radipole and Wareham and rowing clubs at Weymouth, Poole and Christchurch. You may find your ancestor involved in fishing clubs such as at Dorchester or involved in playing bowls at Bridport Bowling Club.

Dorset History Centre holds collections relating to certain sporting clubs. These include Poole Cricket Club, Dorchester Town Football Club, Purbeck Yacht Club and Dorchester Fishing Club. Where clubs still exist today some retain their own archival records so it's worth contacting them for information. Newspaper reports are a great way of finding out more about your ancestors sporting activities, including any competitions they entered. You may find relevant results by simply entering your ancestor's name into an online search and the lucky ones amongst you may even find a photograph published. Reports can be short giving few details and no names; alternatively they can be lengthy, naming everyone who took part. One example from the *Poole and South-Western Herald* dated 23 Jun 1864 describes a cricket match that took place between Poole and Wareham the previous Wednesday. It is noted that the weather was unfavourable, accounting for their low scores, and the match was won by Poole who made 155 runs compared with 115 by Wareham. The scores are given in full as you find today, including the players' surnames.

score of 155 against ...

POOLE.

First Innings.

		Second Innings.	
Blanchard, c H. Bennett, b F. Squires	3	c and b Dean	15
Oakley, b F. Squires	4	b Dean	1
Dunford, b F. Squires	21	not out	9
Rickman, b Bayley	7	run out	4
Stone, b Bayley	7	c Bennett, b Dean	7
Rollings, b F. Squires	0	c Elmes, b Squires	0
Viant, c Capel, b Bayley	1	c Elmes, b Bayley	0
George, b Bayley	11	c Elmes, b Squires	2
Hurdle, c Capel, b Bayley	0	c Smith, b Squires	7
Sutherland, c Smith, b Squires	6	b Squires	1
Gosse, not out	1	b Bayley	0
Byes, 13; wides, 8	21	byes, 16; wides, 11	27
Total	**82**	**Total**	**73**

63. Poole's results from the Poole v. Wareham cricket match, 1864.

Heraldry

Heraldry is the study of coats of arms, how they are passed down through generations and what each feature on the arms symbolises. It is a vast topic and you could spend a lifetime studying it, but just knowing some of the basics may help your research. You often see coats of arms in tourist shops, where they attempt to sell items such as coasters and magnets to customers who wish to purchase an item bearing their name. But arms are not associated by surname. One surname can be associated with many different arms, as they can have multiple points of origin. A majority of public online family trees featuring coats of arms are incorrect, with people assuming arms belong to their family. They also change through generations, with different symbols and dissections added to the shield to represent different generations and intermarriage. If you believe your ancestors held the right to bear a coat of arms, start with *Burke's General Armory of England, Scotland, Ireland and Wales* which features an alphabetical list of armigers. This is freely available online. Where your family has previously had the right to bear arms, then you are more likely to be able to trace your tree back further, with pedigrees provided to heralds by people in order to prove their right to the arms. Today, the right to bear arms still exists and new arms are still being created. This is policed by the College of Arms.

Estate Records

When speaking to Luke Dady and Jacqui Halewood from Dorset History Centre, they felt that estate records were often overlooked by genealogists. The archive holds a wealth of estate documentation including the Bankes estate of Kingston Lacy and Corfe Castle, the Chantmarle Manor Estate and the Glyn estate amongst many others. There are some estates within Dorset which are owned by colleges such as the Bincombe Estate which belongs to the Caius College, Cambridge. Dorset History Centre still holds many of these college-owned records, such as some for Bincombe estate for the dates 1829 -1947.

Estate records comprise title deeds, maps, marriage settlements, photographs, letters and family papers. You may find yourself accessing estate records without realising it through searching the archives catalogue for your ancestor. It is not always obvious where to find estate records. The intermarriages of the landed gentry meant that estates can own land in different counties, so the records associated with each estate can end up in archives all over the UK. The Dorset and Somerset Estate of the Marquis of Anglesey, held at Dorset History Centre include title deeds from Devon and Cornwall. The records of these family-owned estates are interesting to anyone with ancestors who lived within these estate boundaries, not just those related to the families who owned them.

Photographs

There is nothing quite like finding a photograph of an ancestor for the first time. Being able to put a face to the story is exciting and rewarding. It is important to gain as much information from a photograph as you can. This will involve looking at what people are wearing which can help to date the photograph; the clothes can tell us other information such as their financial status, military involvement or employment. Look closely to see if you can spot any jewellery, medals or badges that might provide a clue to a story. Hairstyles and facial hair can also help to date a photograph. Notice if there is anything of interest in the background, such as a landmark, family pet or an heirloom.

We all have photographs of unidentified people and experience the frustration of not knowing which relative, if any, are shown. It is easier to identify people from a group family photograph when you can work out who people are according to their apparent ages. It is important not to blindly guess who a person may be. People retained photographs of their friends, colleagues and neighbours so don't assume that you are definitely related to this person. All you can do is gather all of the information that you can from the image and retain it in the hope that further down the line of your research, you may come across something or someone who can help you to prove who the person is.

If you are the lucky owner of family photographs, make sure you get them scanned in and saved to at least two places to prevent loss. And most importantly, once you know who they are, make a note on your scanned copy and on the back of the photo itself – in pencil.

If you are happy to share these images with others, upload them to your online

64. *Eliza Ann Percey (nee Toms) with four of her children in 1898. Believed to have been taken in Bradford Peverell but the background gives few clues.*

family tree so that others can see their ancestor's faces too. If you are struggling to find a photograph for someone, there are a few places to try. The best option to try first is to contact any relatives who may possess a photograph. You may also find a photograph in newspapers, criminal records, in archives, attached to other people's online trees or via social media. I recently found a photograph of my great-grand-father's sister on a Facebook page dedicated to the parish the family resided in. As well as photographs of people, don't underestimate the interest in viewing photographs of places. Seeing an historic photograph of a village where our ancestor resided at the time they lived there can help us to see the world through their eyes.

65. My father Rodney Osmond as a boy around 1960.

Other Records

Dorset History Centre hold a vast collection of records relating to Women's Institutes across the county, certain political groups such as the Bridport Conservative Club and local government records. Try to be creative in your thinking as to what records may relate to your ancestor and where they may be found. Records such as these surrounding social groups are rarely catalogued by each individual's name.

CHAPTER 17

Internet Sources and Social Media

We should consider ourselves very lucky to live in a time where we have access to the internet. Undoubtedly it has its negative points, but for us genealogists, the internet opens up a whole new avenue of research. We can access documents from home without the need to travel; we can contact cousins via social media and messaging services; we can use search engines to find photographs of people and places, and we can join online groups of people who share an interest, whether it is a surname study group or a local history group.

This chapter will look at a range of possible online sources that we can use, although the list is by no means exhaustive. New websites and groups are being created every day and more records and transcriptions are uploaded frequently. As well as those mentioned below, don't forget to visit the websites belonging to Dorset History Centre, the National Archives and local museums for further information.

Genealogy Subscription Websites

Websites such as Ancestry, FindMyPast, The Genealogist and My Heritage offer subscribers an increasing number of records. Each website has a range of subscription options depending on the records you wish to view. For example, you will need a worldwide membership if you need to search relatives overseas; if you wish to search newspapers on FindMyPast, you will currently need their 'Pro' membership. Each website has overlaps of records, such as census records, as well as records unique to the website. It can be an advantage to have a membership of more than one website in order to have access to the all collections you wish to search.

Before rushing to pay membership to a particular website, search for each company's online record collections. This can help you to avoid paying for a website that does not have any extra records than you need; by researching their current collections you can gain a sense of what is best for you. The Genealogist has an excellent collection of maps which will interest you if you had land-owning relatives. Ancestry has collections of Dorset records, including parish registers and Dorchester prison records. FindMyPast often receives exclusive rights to major records such as the 1921 census and it was also the first to publish the 1939 register. MyHeritage has many advanced features for helping customers to analyse their DNA results, including AutoCluster and a Chromosome browser.

As well as the records it holds, you should research other features of the websites that may appeal to you. They each have their own online tree-building facility, where you can also upload an existing tree from another site or program as a GEDCOM file. Certain layouts of these trees may appeal to you more than others. Some websites, such as Ancestry, allow you to link your DNA results to your family tree, allowing a much greater and more reliable research experience. Ancestry and FindMyPast also have a messaging service where you can contact other members about a shared family tree. If you are new to genealogy, why not start with a free trial offer to a particular site; this way you can get a flavour of how to use the website and then decide if it is right for you.

Websites such as Ancestry and FindMyPast provide a 'hints' feature. Whilst this can sometimes be helpful and alert you to relevant records, at other times the hints are unfortunately false. Accepting a false hint will lead you into a minefield of errors as you attach other irrelevant records and build a completely incorrect history for your ancestor! *Never* trust a record that has been supplied to you through the Hints feature without checking it thoroughly. In addition, never blindly trust another person's family tree. I really cannot stress this enough; I have seen so many errors on other people's family trees and these are sadly copied from person to person. This is *not* how genealogy works. We can only research our family history through thorough record checking and proper research.

OPC Dorset
Mentioned several times throughout this book is the Dorset Online Parish Clerk website, found at www.opcdorset.org. The homepage features links to every Dorset parish, with each place having its own page. Each town and village page varies from having a small number of records to having their own externally hosted site with hundreds of records. Generally, each standard page features a photograph of the parish church alongside a brief history of the area. The name of the volunteer attributed to researching the parish is given, together with their email address. Below this are the records that have been transcribed by volunteers. Whilst many counties have OPC pages, the one for Dorset is of the highest calibre, being frequently updated with new records that are all freely available.

Unfortunately, some parishes do not have a volunteer assigned to them. In these cases, records which have previously been transcribed still appear and there is a note asking for a new volunteer to take over and transcribe further records. If you have some free time and enjoy reading older documents, think about signing up. The work that is transcribed helps countless numbers of people around the world who are researching their Dorset ancestors. You may even come across new records that help you with your own family tree.

As the records on this website are transcriptions, it is still strongly advised to

Census	1841 Census [Keith Searson]
	1851 Census [Royston Clarke]
	1861 Census [John Ridout]
	1871 Census [John Ridout]
	1881 Census [Terry Smith]
	1891 Census [John Ridout]
	1901 Census
	1911 Census
Parish Registers	Baptisms 1732-1880 [Barbara Hunt]
	Marriages 1710-1812, 1732-1842 [Peter Collins, Barbara Hunt]
	Burials 1732-1880 [Barbara Hunt]

66. Snippet of the OPC Dorset page for Wraxall. The volunteers' names are given in brackets.

view the original record where possible. This is the same for any website, including paid subscription genealogy websites, whose records are transcriptions only. This is so that you can check for any errors in transcription and ensure that no additional information was missed. These transcriptions are of huge benefit and can save us time in locating a particular record in the archive when we know precisely where to find it.

Town and Village Websites

Bere Regis History Menu

Find a word on this page...

Murder Of Priscilla Brown

Bere Regis Manor

Bere Regis Methodist Chapel

The Village in the BBC WW2 Peoples War Archive

Village Charities from 1646 onwards

History of the Village Schools from 1846 onwards

The Great Storm 1987

Historic Maps of Dorset & The Bere Regis Area

Murders in the village...

Ancient History of the Village...

Village Archaeological Notes

Bere Regis Industries from 1335 onwards

Directory of Bere Regis Listed Buildings

PigotsTrade Directories 1830 - 1939

67. A selection of some of the historical records available on the Bere Regis website.

Many towns and villages have their own websites. These are generally full of contemporary news and events, but often they have pages linked to local history and records of genealogical interest. Try carrying out a search for the parish of interest to you to see what results are returned. My father currently hosts the Bere Regis village website at www.bereregis.org, which has hundreds of records and transcriptions of interest to those with ancestors in the area, including hearth tax returns, maps and wills. There is a website for Sutton Poyntz at www.suttonpoyntz.org.uk, where you can view maps and read a comprehensive village history relating to each property. There are also excellent websites for Kingston (www.kingstonopc.org.uk), East Lulworth (www.eastlulworth.org.uk) and Verwood (www.verwoodhistorical.org), amongst others.

Social Media
Signing up to different social media sites can result in many surprise findings which can help your research. Don't feel you have to set up your own updated page if you do not wish to do so; just by signing up and having a fairly empty account you will be able to access the information available. Instagram is a great resource for images. You can either choose to search by a name term across multiple accounts; for example, searching for 'Blacksmith' or 'Piddlehinton' will bring up images related to these terms, where they have been tagged appropriately. The danger of doing this is you will receive numerous results which may be of little interest to you. The best way of using Instagram is to 'follow' pages of interest. You can choose to follow professional genealogy accounts, those linked to a particular village or groups dedicated to Dorset history. You will then receive updates on your main page every time a group you follow posts a new image.

Facebook has a similar system where groups have pages dedicated to county history, the history of a particular parish, surname history or general genealogy research. Again by following pages of interest to you, you will receive updates on their new posts. Facebook uses more text than Instagram and this allows users to post stories and transcriptions. You can sign up to various genealogy research interest groups where users can ask for help on a particular brick wall they are facing or get in contact with others who are researching the same parish or family as you. Consider following official pages belonging to archives and subscription sites which will keep you updated with new online collection releases.

Social media sites, as well as messaging services on genealogy sites, allow us to contact individuals, including family members we have lost contact with or new-found cousins discovered through DNA testing. If you choose to message someone like this through social media, it is best to keep the contact brief at first, and do not get too upset if you do not get a response. Not everybody will have the same degree of interest in family history and some may be hoping *not* to unravel family secrets. Tread carefully and respect people's privacy. Some people do not visit their accounts regularly and you may receive a response many months, or even years, after you have contacted them.

Professional Genealogists' Websites

When undertaking your own family history research, you may find that you would benefit from some professional assistance. Hiring a professional genealogist can be of great benefit; they can source specific records for you relating to your ancestors, help you to interpret them and give you pointers as to what further research could be done. There are several genealogists available to hire, all specializing in different areas; check out their websites for details. The website for my business, The Past Revealed (www.thepastrevealed.co.uk), features an Ancestor of the Month blog to inspire others to research their family stories.

Sarah Tucker Bugden 1825 - 1877

My fourth-great grandmother Sarah was born in 1825 to Wesleyan Methodist parents, Robert and Elizabeth Bugden. She was later baptised into the Church of England alongside her brother and sister in Poole, Dorset in 1828. The family moved

68. A snapshot of my Ancestor of the Month blog on my website for 'The Past Revealed'.

Other Websites of Interest

Family Search (www.familysearch.org) is run by the Church of Jesus Christ of Latter-Day Saints and comprises free records and transcriptions. You will need an account to view results of searches but it is a free service. It features a range of international records, as well as British documents, including Dorset Parish Registers transcriptions for 1538 -2001.

The Guild of One-Name Studies (https://one-name.org) features over 8000 different surname studies. Rather than being particularly genealogy-based, these studies are based purely on one surname, although this can inherently help us with genealogical research. The surnames are the more uncommon names - obviously studying names like Smith or Taylor would be more than a lifetime's work! Some Dorset surnames featured here include Hansford and Hackett.

Cyndi's List, is run by Cyndi Ingle in Washington, USA and (www.cyndislist. com) comprises a list of useful genealogy links to other websites with daily updates as to what collections have been added to websites around the world. It is free to use and you can browse categories alphabetically from adoption to wills and probate.

A Vision of Britain through Time (www.visionofbritain.org.uk) has pages for each parish, giving statistics, interesting facts and maps for each area. It is a great website to use if you have come across an unfamiliar area within your research. If you type in Marnhull as an example, the site gives us an extract from an 1870 Gazetteer, alongside an old map. There are also links to Marnhull's entry on Wikipedia, GENUKI and GeoNames websites.

GenGuide (www.genguide.co.uk) was founded by Peter Humphries and is an excellent resource to discover more about different genealogical sources. The site is easy to use and the language is accessible even if you are just starting to trace your family tree. If you have any queries about an historic source, check on GenGuide to find out more about it. Information includes background information, where the document can be found and the dates that each source covers. There are also reading suggestions and website links to relevant information.

Free UK Genealogy is a charity organisation comprising three volunteer transcription sites. These are **FreeREG** (www.freereg.org.uk) which focuses on parish register and nonconformist register entries, **FreeBMD** (www.freebmd. org.uk) which looks at civil registration indexes and **FreeCEN** (www.freecen.org.uk) which concentrates on UK census entries.

The website is significant, not least because the information is all available for free, but also because it contains such a large amount of information. FreeREG currently has over 53 million records, FreeCEN has over 42 million records and FreeBMD has 374 million records. These numbers increase every day. These websites often include details that other websites do not include in their transcriptions so are definitely worth checking.

The **British Film Institute's** National Archive (www.bfi.org.uk/bfi-national-archive) has over 12,000 historic films available to watch for free, dating back to around 1895. You can use this to search parishes where your ancestors lived at the time, or their occupation to find an example of how they worked. Results include village fairs, sports matches, street life, circus performers and early amateur and professional dramatics. If you are lucky, you may even be able to find a film which shows your ancestors, most of whom will not be searchable by name via BFI. Some examples of films from Dorset include Verwood potters in 1912, Dorchester celebrating their Brewery Centenary in 1937, Dorset County Fair in 1963 and Stoll Bailey's 1925 film taken along the Dorset coast, showing Lulworth Cove and Durdle Door.

CHAPTER 18

Family History Societies

If you are not yet a member of a Family History Society (FHS), it is definitely worth considering because for a small annual fee, you receive benefits such as access to resources and materials, networking with others with the same interest and the receipt of a regular journal. The main two FHS of interest are 'Dorset Family History Society' and 'Somerset & Dorset Family History Society'. To see if either or both of these are of interest to you, have a look at their respective websites to see what they can offer. The majority of societies are county-based, although there are exceptions which may be of interest to you depending on your family's background, such as the Catholic Family History Society, the Anglo-Italian Family History Society and the Huguenot Society of Britain and Ireland. Generally run by volunteers, Family History Societies are a very worthwhile means of meeting other family historians and furthering your research. At the time of writing, opening times of most FHS are rather restricted due to the coronavirus pandemic, so do check their websites for their current opening times to avoid a wasted trip to societies' research centres.

Dorset Family History Society
Treetops Research Centre
Suite 5 Stanley House
3 Fleets Lane
Poole
Dorset
BH15 3AJ
www.dorsetfhs.org.uk
01202 785623

The website for Dorset FHS provides many useful links for those researching in the county and beyond, a schedule of workshops and a well-stocked shop where you can purchase books, DVDs, CDs and maps dating from the late nineteenth century/early twentieth century, as well as parish records, indexes to newspapers and school logbooks to name but a few.

A research service is available for an hourly fee and there are Zoom chats or phone calls to assist you. They also hold monthly meetings and computer group meetings.

Visitors are welcome at Treetops Research Centre in Poole where volunteers are on hand to assist all researchers, not just those looking for Dorset ancestors.

Open to everyone (including non-members) Mondays, Wednesdays and Saturdays 10am-3pm for only £3 a visit. Access major internet websites, early censuses and parish registers. You can see what transcriptions the Society holds for each parish through a free online search which lists the years transcribed for baptisms, marriages and burials. There is a research and lending library, sales area and extensive research material to assist you.

Membership is £15 (£19 overseas) and includes quarterly journals, computer group meetings and access to members' surname interests in the members' only area on the website. All details of what they offer and any other information can be found on the website.

With thanks to Sheila Martin, Secretary of Dorset FHS for the above.

Somerset & Dorset Family History Society
Broadway House, Peter Street, Yeovil, Somerset. BA20 1PN
https://sdfhs.org/
sdfhs@btconnect.com
01935 429609

The Somerset & Dorset Family History Society has eight groups based across the two counties. In Dorset there are groups for the Blackmore Vale which meets at Sturminster Newton, East Dorset which meets at Wimborne, West Dorset which meets at Loders and South Dorset which meets at Weymouth. Viewing the webpage for each area displays what talks or events are organised for the coming months in the region.

On their website, there is a free search function for headstones in the county, with members receiving a more detailed description. For free you can still see the deceased's name, year of death, age, any relationship stated on the stone, the parish in which the headstone is found and the denomination of the burial ground. This is a great help for tracking down the real thing in person. As well as these memorial inscriptions, the Society organises a variety of other transcription projects from time to time including marriages and burials for Dorset. The Society is also manning a photographic project whereby people are invited to send in photographs of their named ancestors for introduction into a database that can be used by other researchers. As this database grows, it will undoubtedly become a key resource for genealogists who wish to see the faces of their ancestors.

Their online shop has many genealogy books as well as a selection of CDs such as the Dorset Methodist Centenary Roll, poor law records for Lytchett Matravers and Bradford Abbas' parish records. A much wider variety of Dorset parish registers are available to purchase in booklet format. There is a small selection of maps to buy and a range of other record transcriptions offered, including the listing of hemp and flax growers 1782-1793.

Their HQ in Yeovil holds pedigrees that have been deposited by other researchers as well as a library of many relevant publications. These include a large number of out-of-print books that can greatly help with genealogical research and the social history of the area; you can search their library holdings via their website. On hand to help are the society's research volunteers who possess a wealth of knowledge and great enthusiasm for the subject. For a small fee they can also answer enquiries for those who are unable to visit in person.

Benefits of becoming a member of the Society include a quarterly journal and priority access to their onsite research facilities. New members receive a free hour of research on site. If you are not a member you may still use their research facilities in Yeovil at a cost of £3 per day and you are also able to attend their talks and events. At the time of writing, an annual UK subscription costs £18, with an overseas annual subscription costing £22.

With thanks to Rita Pettet, Chairman of Somerset & Dorset FHS for the above.

Family History Federation

www.familyhistoryfederation.com   01263 824951

The Family History Federation is an educational charity which promotes the membership of Family History Societies. They advertise upcoming talks and events given by societies across the country. They also provide educational factsheets and have a list of many useful free websites including links to help read old handwriting and how to translate basic Latin. It is worth seeing what talks are offered by other family history societies based in other counties as these are often of general interest rather than being at county-level, with topics sometimes based on different occupations. Their website lists all the accredited Family History Societies in the country, as well as groups based on surname studies and some societies based abroad.

The Family History Federation has two fantastic shops. The first is Family History Books Online, which as you would expect sells a wide range of publications. These can be searched by title, author or category. Alternatively, you may simply choose to browse the books for sale which can be a good way of coming across an unexpectedly useful title. The Federation's other shop is called the Parish Chest. Here you can choose to search for publications from a particular society, carry out a wide search of all societies offerings or browse by category. This website is expanding fast so don't miss out!

The Family History Federation's 'Really Useful Family History Show' is an online event with virtual talks from genealogy experts, workshops to develop research skills and one-to-one sessions with accredited genealogists who can offer help and advice regarding your family tree research. The show is currently an annual event with a small fee for registering to attend. If you are interested, have a look at the dedicated website (www.fhf-reallyuseful.com). Some of the talks are free!

The Federation also produces the Really Useful Podcast series. These are focused on relevant genealogy topics such as social media and the 1939 Register, and provide another means of learning about the best practice of research. They are available to listen to via the Federation's website.

If your society would like to join the Federation, joining is easy; you just have to complete an online form available on their website. There are conditions of membership, such as having a membership of at least ten people and having existed for at least one year. The benefits of joining include free publicity being advertised on their website and at the Federation's events, Public Liability Insurance and advice to societies regarding relevant issues such as data protection and copyright queries. They also have a range of help sheets and advice on research. Your society could also gain by having opportunities of their arrangements selling your products online via Parish Chest.

Other Societies

You may wish to join a FHS based in another county, depending on where your ancestors lived. It is very rare that a person's family tree will be based all within one county, so branch out and look at other FHS websites to see what they could offer you. They all vary in terms of resources and membership benefits.

You may also find it worthwhile to join a local history society. Some people like to join the one for the area where they live, even if their own ancestors are not from the area. This can sometimes help us to feel more 'at home' with the local history and may lead you to research other people's family trees or your house history. There are many local history groups in Dorset, most of which are listed on the British Association for Local History's website at www.balh.org.uk. Examples include the Cerne Historical Society, Highcliffe History Society and Bryanston Village History Group. Whilst these are not strictly based around genealogical research, they will undoubtedly be useful to you in terms of historical context.

CHAPTER 19
Using the Archives

As we have seen throughout these chapters it is impossible to thoroughly research your family tree without visiting local archives. While many records have been digitised to be available online, many need to be viewed at the archives. For some people this may be inconvenient, time-consuming and perhaps expensive if it involves travelling, but the feeling of viewing a paper record makes the experience more worthwhile than simply seeing a scanned record online. You can even potentially hold records that your ancestors once did and upon which they made their mark! Most importantly, you can view records that are unique to the archives and cannot be found elsewhere.

Visiting the archives for the first time can be a daunting experience, but rest assured that we were all first-timers once, and after the first visit you will feel much more confident and eager to return. This chapter provides guidance regarding the local archives related to Dorset and the surrounding area. Do remember to check on opening times as these can change; and you will also usually need to contact the archives in advance to book your place for the day.

General Rules
Check each archives website prior to your visit as they each have slightly different rules regarding visiting and what is allowed to be taken in with you. Generally speaking, the following rules apply:
- Personal bags to be left in a locker
- No food or drink allowed in the archive
- Pens are not allowed but visitors may use a pencil - this is to protect any permanent damage being caused to irreplaceable documents.
- Cameras, tablets and camera phones are usually allowed to be used for an extra fee. Ask at reception on your arrival about purchasing a photo pass

Always view the archives catalogue online before you visit. Make a list of all the records that you wish to view including their reference number. This will save you time when you arrive and give you more time to view the records. A small selection of records can usually be booked in advance of your visit so they will be ready for you when you arrive.

During your visit, note down every record you have viewed and any information it contains. This will save you from ordering the same record again by mistake in the future, or needing to order it again if you failed to note down any information.

If you are viewing a large book, such as a school register, use the provided cushions to protect the spine.

If you have any questions, ask the staff - they are all there to help you get the most out of your visit.

Be aware that not all documents are catalogued by name. For example, some parish records are listed according to people's names such as 'Bastardy Order of Mary Greene'. Others will not be catalogued by name and these can easily be missed despite being relevant; for example, a record may be recorded as 'Vestry Minutes of Stalbridge', with no names given of those included. In these cases, the record will need to be viewed to see if it contains relevant information for you - this is time-consuming but well worth it.

If you cannot visit the archives in person, you can choose to pay for their research services. Using this service, the archive staff will send you scanned copies of the records you are interested in, but there is a fee for this service and sometimes a bit of a wait to receive the results by email.

Dorset History Centre

Dorset History Centre is the most likely archives you will visit as they hold the majority of the records relevant to Dorset. It is located at Bridport Road, Dorchester, DT1 1RP, next to the Keep Military Museum, with a car park a very short walk away. Located within the town centre, it is close to several shops and cafes should you wish to have some lunch during your visit. Dorchester has excellent public transport links with regular buses and trains.

Among their collection, Dorset History Centre hold local newspapers, parish registers, school records, probate records, maps, electoral registers and photo-graphs. There is a selection of private correspondence, business records, court records and an important collection of oral history relating to the county.

Dorset History Centre is also excellent for providing more generic information about the county and specific parishes of interest which can help to give you an idea of the environment in which your ancestors lived. They have records of local societies too such as political associations and sporting groups.

The local studies library at Dorset History Centre holds around 15,000 books and journals. These can all be viewed at the library but cannot be 'taken out' as you can at other public lending libraries; this is entirely justified and understandable as many of the books are rare. The rarest of these books are available to view on request and are not held on the open access shelving. The subject matter of all the books is all relevant to the centre, with categories of interest to genealogists including Dorset history, published family histories and military history. Relevant journals available to view here include the Journal of the Dorset Family History Society and Dorset County Magazine.

Southampton Archives

It is good practice to check the holdings of other local archives if Dorset History Centre does not have a record that you require; other archives may hold relevant other documents of interest. Southampton Archives is located at the Civic Centre, Civic Centre Road, Southampton, SO14 7LY, in the city centre. As the name suggests, the archives focuses largely on records relevant to Southampton, however, it holds many records originating from Dorset.

The archive holds Dorchester Apprenticeship Indentures for 1770 -1795. These include people living within the Dorchester region as well as those from further afield who were apprenticed in the area. There are also records relating to Dorset orphans who were assisted by local charities and a small selection of Dorset title deeds. Miscellaneous records include mentions of Dorset people recorded in Quarter Sessions records, crew lists and business records.

Wiltshire & Swindon History Centre

Located a short walk from the train station at Cocklebury Road, Chippenham, Wiltshire, SN15 3QN, the Wiltshire & Swindon History Centre has its own car park and is a ten-minute walk from the town centre. As well as having the expected records related to Wiltshire such as parish registers, court records and newspapers, the archive also has many records relating to Dorset.

Amongst the records relating to Dorset are documents relating to Dorset parishes involved in the Salisbury Methodist Circuit, such as Cranborne and Edmondsham, a selection of title deeds and a large number of records relating to parishes that come under the Diocese of Salisbury. These include documents relating to presentments, church repairs and cemetery extensions. A notable collection is the probate records relating to several Dorset parishes and listed in the Probate chapter of this book.

There are numerous other specific records of interest to those researching Dorset ancestors. If searching for a person's name does not yield any results, often the best way to find records is to enter the name of the parish you are interested in to see if there are any results. Searching their catalogue for the Dorset parish of 'Broadoak' yields six results; five relate to church alterations with the remaining result being a marriage settlement between Thomas Pitt and Ann Wilkinson. Looking at the results for Bere Regis, there are forty-two results. Although many records refer to church repairs and changes, there are many people named in the records and other documents of interest. These include a baptismal certificate for the vicar James Young, a nonconformist meeting house certificate and a list of people who failed to attend church in 1663. It is therefore worth spending some time having a search of their catalogue to see if there are any items of interest to your research.

Somerset Heritage Centre

Somerset Heritage Centre is situated at Brunel Way, Norton Fitzwarren, Taunton, TA2 6SF and conveniently has its own free car park. As well as housing the record collections, Somerset Studio Libraries and Somerset Museum Service collections are also stored on the same site making for an interesting visit.

There is a large collection of deeds relating to Dorset held here. Many of these are detailed in their catalogue, with names and parishes given. You can therefore search online for a person or parish of interest to you. There is also a small selection of probate material relating to Dorset people, maps and business records. As you would expect, a majority of Dorset records held at Somerset Heritage Centre relate to parishes to the West of the county towards the border, such as Lyme Regis and Beaminster.

Devon Heritage Centre

Devon Heritage Centre is the main archive for Devon situated at Great Moor House, Bittern Road, Exeter, EX2 7NL, with a separate branch office at North Devon Record Office in Barnstaple. There is a small car park.

As with other archives outside of Dorset, the material related to the county here consists largely of title deeds with some probate documents, quarter sessions minutes and nonconformist records. There are also settlement certificates, removal orders and bastardy bonds - some related to Dorset people. Their catalogue can be searched by name or parish.

Hampshire Archives and Local Studies

Aside from records from the Bournemouth, Poole and Christchurch area, Hampshire Archives has considerably fewer records relating to Dorset than the other archives. Nevertheless, it is important to bear these archives in mind as they could be holding the very record you need! Located in Sussex Street, Winchester, SO23 8TH, it is very close to Winchester train station. There are many car parks that can be used throughout the city.

Again, there are many title deeds held here for properties in Dorset parishes, as well as quarter sessions minutes, estate records and manorial surveys. Other miscellaneous items include artwork of Dorset including Swanage and Portland, personal correspondence and journals.

The National Archives (TNA)

Eventually, you will discover that you need a record from the National Archives. As with all archives, it is not necessary to visit in person and you can opt to pay for their copying service to save time travelling. The National Archives is located at Kew, Richmond, Surrey TW9 4DU next to Kew Gardens Station.

The most likely records you will wish to access from TNA are court records, War Office documents and probate material. Their online catalogue, named Discovery, has an excellent search feature enabling you to search their collections as well as those of other archives throughout England and Wales. You can choose to filter or restrict your search to just specific archives if you wish. Where TNA holds records that are available online, this will be stated. Sometimes there is a fee to be paid via TNA to access this digital record whereas other times you will be directed to view the record on another website, such as Ancestry.

It can help to understand TNA's basic referencing system. For example, reference numbers starting WO relate to the War Office, whereas those starting with C relate to Chancery court records.

There is a large amount of Dorset-related material at TNA. For example, there are nearly 17,000 probate records, over 13,000 Chancery court records and over 12,500 Exchequer court records. They also hold a large collection of Ordnance Survey maps, census returns and other Westminster court documentation. Of the more miscellaneous items, TNA holds registers of Dorset Friendly Societies, a selection of passports and some correspondence. As with all the previously mentioned archives, there is a selection of title deeds, many of which are not indexed by name or parish.

Other Archives

You may find Dorset-related material in any archives across England. The best way to search for these is using TNA's Discovery catalogue so they are all searched at the same time. For example, you may find that a letter written from a Dorset person was posted to Kent and has therefore been archived in Kent History Centre. Other holdings may appear more random, such as Nottingham University Library holding many Dorset deeds, Birmingham Archives Service holding oral history of Dorset folk and Isle of Wight Record Office holding some Dorset manorial records.

CHAPTER 20
Museums of Relevance

Museums are a wonderful resource full of records and objects that can give a unique insight into our ancestors' lives. Information gained may be specific to a person but will usually provide us with a more general knowledge, like the history of a town or an understanding of a person's occupation. Visiting museums is highly worthwhile and something I would always encourage. Having a background in museum work myself, I understand the enthusiasm, passion and knowledge that the staff has regarding their museum topics. Museums are increasingly improving their online access too, with an expanding number of them scanning in documents and photographing collections so that these can be seen via their website.

There are many different museums that may be beneficial for you to visit. These include military museums and heritage sites focused on specific occupations or ways of life, all of which may be found throughout England. An ancestor from Dorset will not necessarily have been based with a Dorset regiment; for example, my husband's Dorset-based grandfather served with the Gordon Highlanders, whose museum is in Aberdeen. Here, we will look at the museums based in Dorset which may be of interest but the list is far from exhaustive.

Dorset Museum

Situated in High West Street in the county town of Dorchester which hosts a range of interesting museums, Dorset Museum is perhaps the best place to visit first to gain a good general knowledge of the county. The site has changed a lot since I served my university work placement there in 2008, but I am glad to see that these changes are all for the better and the museum is going from strength to strength.

Dorset Museum successfully presents the key aspects of the county's history, including galleries on local artists, authors and the natural landscape. Perhaps of most interest to genealogists is the 'People's Dorset' gallery. This tells the story of human history in the county up to the present day and displays a variety of archaeological finds, textiles and artefacts of great interest. This museum ultimately provides a great overview of county life with a good sense of the local culture.

Bridport Museum

Located at 25 South Street, a highlight of Bridport Museum is their collection relating to the rope and net-making industries which were prevalent in the town. The museum runs rope-making demonstrations in the morning on selected days, and these are wonderful for anyone to watch but particularly if your ancestor worked in the trade. This can really bring to life the work involved, rather than simply reading about it. Other collections include fossils, ancient artefacts and shipbuilding. There is a lot to see here regarding our ancestors' occupations, including brewing, baking and fishing.

Poole Museum

Just down from the seafront at 4 High Street in the Old Town area, you will find Poole Museum with its modern frontage and historic interior. The museum is free for all to visit. Whilst there are wonderful exhibits on prehistory, genealogist visitors are more likely to be drawn towards the exhibitions on the maritime industry, occupational history and social history of the town. Much of this will be of interest to those of you with ancestors who worked in the trades featured, but it is an essential visit for those with ancestors from Poole itself. It is worth checking out what temporary exhibitions and events are on before you go. Past exhibitions have looked at gypsy and traveller culture in Poole and events have included a Tudor cooking session.

Blandford Fashion Museum

A much more specialised museum, Blandford Fashion Museum is housed at Lime Tree House, The Plocks in Blandford Forum. The Museum is of great interest to see the types of clothes that our ancestors would have worn, or even created if they worked in the fashion industry. There are informative exhibitions on button-making and glove manufacture. The collection dates from the 1700s to the 1970s. They regularly change their exhibitions meaning repeat visits are recommended in order to see a wider variety of their large collection. Blandford Fashion Museum highlights the link between the costume of the time and the social history that led to their development, with their collection varying in subject. Accessories are also on show, including gloves, shoes, scarves and fans, all of which are beautifully displayed. A particular favourite temporary exhibition from my visit was the wedding dress collection. It is truly a remarkable experience to view these clothes up close to see the workmanship that went into their creation.

Museum of East Dorset

Formerly known as the Priest's House Museum, the Museum of East Dorset can be found at 23-29 High Street in Wimborne within a Grade II listed building dating from the late 1500s/early 1600s. The museum holds a wealth of local history artefacts and social history collections. The building was previously used as an ironmonger's shop and there is still a display on this today. Other occupational highlights include a Victorian portrait camera and products from Witchampton

Paper Mill. A general social history highlight is their collection of Victorian Valentine's Day cards, which gives a real insight into the celebration at the time. Other objects of interest include toys and clothing from the 1800s onwards.

The Keep Military Museum

Housed in the fantastic historic building of the gatehouse for the Depot Barracks of the Dorsetshire Regiment with the mock appearance of a castle, the Keep Military Museum cannot be missed on Barrack Road. The Keep is the military museum of Dorset and Devon; displays of all the regiments associated with the county lead you through four floors of exhibitions before ending with a fantastic rooftop view over Dorchester. The museum houses military uniforms, weaponry, medals and silverware amongst other war paraphernalia. The exhibitions explain various conflicts through history that your ancestors may have been involved in and bring this history to life with associated objects on display.

Other Museums of Note

If you are researching military ancestry in the county you may be interested in visiting the Royal Signals Museum on Blandford Camp, Nothe Fort in Weymouth and the Tank Museum on Bovington Camp. Other town museums of interest include Red House Museum in Christchurch, Sherborne Museum, Lyme Regis Museum, Portland Museum, Wareham Town Museum and Blandford Town Museum. There are many others that may be of interest to you, so it is worth investigating what museums are located near the parish where your ancestors were. Visit the Dorset Museums Association website (www.dorsetmuseums.co.uk) to see what other museums are in the county that may be relevant to your research.

CHAPTER 21

Visiting Dorset Parishes

Some people researching their Dorset ancestors will never have visited the county itself; I myself have ancestors from Kent but have yet to visit. Others will be very familiar with Dorset, may have lived there all their lives and will proudly boast they are 'born and bred' there. Whichever description fits you, it is good to know how to make the most out of visiting towns and villages where your ancestors lived, but bear in mind they will have changed considerably over the years.

No doubt much of our family history is learnt through researching records, whether online or in archives, but don't underestimate the value of actually visiting the places where your family once lived. Walking the routes that they once did from home to get to work, to church or other relatives' houses can give an idea of what they saw along the way and the distance they travelled. You can gain a great sense of belonging and have a pleasant day visiting the churches, pubs and local walks that our ancestors once enjoyed. If you do choose to visit a parish, it is best to do your research in advance, noting what sites in particular applied to your ancestors. Don't forget to take any copies of relevant historic maps with you.

Churches

Churches were at the heart of our ancestors' lives far more so than they are for a majority of people today. They attended baptisms, weddings and burials here and even our nonconformist ancestors would have found themselves at their Church of England parish church during their lifetime. Visiting their church gives us the opportunity to see the structure that they saw and revel in the atmosphere, knowing that we can stand where they witnessed significant moments in their life. For those of you with a particularly keen interest, you can research the individual church history to understand what changes have occurred since your ancestors' time there. For example, you may find that the font has moved location since they were baptised. Whilst there, don't forget to look at any tombs or plaques within the church.

Churchyards and Cemeteries

Visiting the place where our ancestors have been buried has obvious advantages. As mentioned in the Memorial Inscriptions chapter, if you can find the gravestone belonging to your forebears you may be able to discover new information about them such as their death date, age and previously unknown family members.

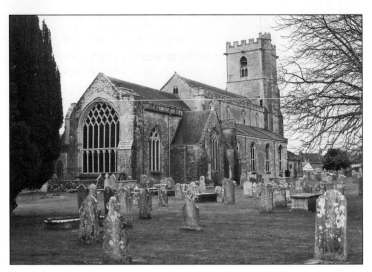
69. *The stunning church of Lady St. Mary in Wareham.*

Unfortunately, a majority of people will find their ancestor has no surviving headstone and may even never have had one created. If you know from burial records the parish in which they were buried, it is worth contacting the relevant church or authority to see if they hold any burial plot plans. These will enable you to find their plot and pay your respects. Some people leave flowers. Where no headstone survives, many people purchase a headstone to mark their ancestor's plot. Many find a comfort in visiting their ancestor's burial location, knowing that their families would have visited them here for many years.

70. *Preston churchyard.*

Homes

Viewing the homes of our ancestors can give a great insight into their lives, seeing the size of the house and appreciating their surroundings. It is not always easy to gain a sense of how things were for them, and the further back in time you go, the harder it is to imagine what the area would have looked like. Tracing house history is a separate subject in itself and care needs to be taken to ensure you are visiting the right house. House numbers and names changed over time and before house numbers were allocated, houses are often described very generically as to their place in the parish. Use every available source to you such as the 1910 Lloyd George Domesday Maps, tithe maps and title deeds in order to make sure the house you are looking at is indeed the right house. When you are confident you have found the correct house, or indeed the plot upon which it once stood, it can help to view maps from the time of their residency to gain an idea of their local surroundings at the time they were there. If the house still stands today, remember to respect the privacy of those who live in it today and bear in mind the house may have changed considerably since your forebears lived there.

Pubs

The local parish pub is likely to have been visited by your ancestors. In small villages where there are only one or two pubs, it is a good afternoon out to visit the local haunts and have a drink or a meal. In larger parishes and towns, there were often many pubs and it may not be possible to know which ones your relatives visited. As with today, the nearest pub to us is not always the one we visit the most. You may find it more relevant if you discover one of your ancestors worked in the local pub. They may be described as a victualler or public house owner; this was a common occupation due to the higher number of pubs then compared with today. I myself have had a drink in a pub where my ancestor worked for several years and it's a truly special feeling.

Farms and Other Occupational Sites

With ancestors from Dorset, you are more than likely to have agricultural labourers and farm workers in your family tree. I found it particularly heart-warming to visit the farms and fields where my family worked in Sutton Poyntz and Bincombe. Both are such beautiful areas and it was lovely to imagine them hard at work in days gone by. Many key features of the landscape will remain unchanged, but you may want to consider viewing tithe maps and enclosure maps to see what has changed.

Farming practices and landscape changes are difficult to imagine today but maps help us to see the changes to the field systems. Try and visit other places where your ancestors worked - pubs, factories and railway stations. It can be quite rewarding!

Other Places of Interest

To gain the best sense of the environment where your ancestor lived when visiting their parish, it helps to know what facilities were in the area at the time and any buildings that were important to them in their lifetime. This may include nonconformist chapels, schools, the town hall, prisons and the local shop. If your ancestor was convicted of an offence or was the victim of a crime, it is worth visiting where the crime took place to see for yourself.

Make a note of any key features in the area that may be unchanged, such as archaeological sites or noticeable features in the landscape. Noting the distance between these sites, you can imagine how they would have moved between them and what routes they would have taken, with a rough time of how long this would have taken them. If you have any old photographs of the area, it may help to take these with you to see the changes first hand.

71. *Custom House, Poole.*

CHAPTER 22
Dorset Surnames

What makes a surname a Dorset surname? Well, with many surnames it can prove difficult to discover their origins. A majority of people in the south of England had hereditary surnames by 1350 and many have multiple origins. There are several different types of surname, listed as follows:

Surname Type	Surname Origin	Surname Examples
Patronymic / Matronymic	Surname originating from a person's father's name (Patronymic) or mother's name (Matronymic)	Davidson, Richards, Matthew
Topographical	Surname taken from a feature of the landscape	Atwell, Byfield, Underwood
Characteristic	Those named after a physical feature or aspect of their personality	Short, Strong, Wise
Occupational	People named after their work	Smith, Wright, Taylor
Habitational	Surname derived from a place name	Brownsea, Sherborne, Manston

Looking at the above list, it is easy to see how one name can originate from multiple places and why some surnames, such as Smith, are so common. In the 1881 census, the top three surnames in Dorset were White, Smith and Brown. These are incredibly common surnames and are certainly not unique to the area. If you meet somebody with the surname White, you cannot tell which area of the country their ancestors were. Other surnames, however, are more unique to Dorset and to the south and these are what we can call 'Dorset surnames'. Some surnames can be conclusively proved as to where they first appeared in the country, whereas others seem to originate from a more general area.

Historians often look at documents such as the hearth tax returns or oath lists in order to map where certain surnames are found. It is possible to do this with a variety of documents over time to map out how people with a certain name moved throughout the country. But not all names have a clear meaning as to their origin. For example, the surname Pheasant may have been adopted by someone who worked with pheasants or who shared a characteristic with the bird.

Surname Anomalies

There is a great interest amongst many family historians in tracing the history of their surname. From my experience, I find it is best not to get too attached to this idea. Whilst many people successfully trace their tree and the derivation of a particular name back for centuries, others will discover that names have been passed down in a somewhat less traditional manner. This may happen through the use of aliases, adoption or the changing of name for reasoning that is never quite clear.

I have two examples close to home. My birth surname is Osmond, a name steeped in heritage in the south. However, my paternal great-great-grandfather was actually born in London with a different surname to an unwed mother and he was subsequently adopted in the south by the Osmond family. My husband's name of O'Shea also fails to be traced back very far. His grandfather was again born to an unwed mother and he took on the surname of his stepfather as a child. It is more common than you might think to find surnames changing.

You may want to consider the surnames that you choose to research and which are important to you. Most frequently, people choose to research their birth name or perhaps their mother's maiden name or a grandparent's name if it is more unusual.

You should be aware that names given on certificates are not always correct. A married woman who has had a child through an affair may simply put her husband's name on the child's birth certificate or parish register as the father, leading us to research the wrong line. This is often proven through DNA testing for more recent connections but is unfortunately sometimes impossible to prove once you get too far back in time.

Illegitimate births are also common to find in family trees, with the father's name often being hard or impossible to discover. There are a surprising number of people who changed their name, sometimes using several aliases for reasons that remain undiscovered. This is often seen with criminals who try to evade the law but for many the reason is not obvious. It may be that they were trying to avoid association towards a 'bad' relative who shared their name or wished to make a new start in a new place with a new name, but this is all conjecture.

Lastly, don't fret when you see the spelling of a surname change. It is only in more recent times that the spelling of surnames has become standardised. Before education and literacy were widespread, the registrar would record a surname however they believed it to be spelt. Our illiterate ancestors were often unaware of how their surname was spelt and this can lead to a large number of variations in a person's lifetime. In my tree I have Osment and Osmond as two separate branches, however, at times the Osment surname is written as Osmond before changing back again. The nature of changing surnames can make it hard to trace certain families whose names change and identification between families of similar surnames can prove challenging. You may be tracing a line of Davison's for generations before it suddenly changes to Davidson. Don't rule a branch out because the name doesn't match exactly with what you believe it to be.

Dorset Surnames

Below you will find a list of Dorset surnames that feature frequently in Dorset or whose origins have been traced back to the county. If your name does not feature on the list, it does not mean it did not originate in the county and I encourage you to do a search into its history if you are interested.

Bowditch – This is a habitational surname from a Dorset estate. The name is most commonly seen in Dorset, Somerset and Devon. In the 1881 census there were 251 people with that surname in Dorset, with Somerset in second place with 122. Most of those with the surname of Bowditch can be seen in parish registers for Thorncombe from the 1500s onwards.

Brickell - There were just 420 Brickells in the 1841 census. The name is overwhelmingly found in Dorset. In the 1881 census, there were 227 Brickells found in the county, with just thirty-two in Hampshire. Most believe the name to be habitational, derived from Great, Little and Bow Brickhill in Buckinghamshire. With early findings of the name being in Buckinghamshire and London, it is possible a family of Brickells settled in Dorset thus spreading the name, as it died out elsewhere.

Bugler – This is thought to be an occupational or descriptive surname for someone who played the bugle, or potentially a habitational name for someone from Bugle in Cornwall. In the 1881 census, 193 Buglers were found in Dorset, followed by thirty-three in Somerset, with seventy-two of those in Dorset being found in Beaminster parish alone. Bugler is first seen in Dorset parish registers in Hazelbury Bryan in 1598.

72. Joane Bugler was buried in Hazelbury Bryan on 9 Oct 1598.

153

Cake - With just 249 in the 1841 England census, this is a fairly rare surname. The origins are occupational for someone who made cakes, although these are not as we recognise them today. Instead, an historic cake-maker made small, flat oval-shaped loaves of bread. Most commonly found in Dorset, the top three parishes for its occurrence in 1881 were Tolpuddle, Wareham St Martin and Bincombe. Early parish register entries are seen in Poole, Church Knowle and Sherborne, with Cakes in the 1641/2 Protestation Oath returns in Winfrith Newburgh.

Coffin - Found most commonly in Hampshire and Dorset, the origins of this surname are debateable. Some believe it derives from the Latin word *calrus* meaning bald, but most believe it describes someone who made baskets known as *coffers*. Parish registers from the 1500s show Coffins in Bere Regis, Stock Gaylard and Lytchett Minster.

Croad - Found in equal measure in Dorset and Hampshire in 1881, this name is thought to have been adopted by those who played a medieval stringed instrument known as a *croude*. The Croads were spread across a range of parishes in 1881 including Melcombe Regis, Alton Pancras and Weymouth. The earliest mention in Dorset parish registers is in Cattistock in 1588 and Sydling St Nicholas in 1602.

Crumpler - Fifty-five per cent of all Crumplers in 1881 were in Dorset, with most in Lytchett Matravers and Wareham Holy Trinity. The earliest parish register entries of the name in Dorset are found in Almer and Sturminster Marshall. The name is characteristic, with *crump* meaning crooked or bent. This name is originally thought to have been given to someone with a hunched posture.

Damon - A surprisingly uncommon name but one which again features most heavily in Dorset. The earliest entry in a parish register in the county is in Abbotsbury in 1583. There is no agreed meaning of the name with some stating it derives from the Greek word *daman* meaning 'to kill', while others believe it originates from German; some also claim the name is patronymic, meaning the son of Damian.

Dominey - Most commonly seen in Dorset and Hampshire, this surname has many spelling variants. The 1881 census shows the name featured most heavily in Iwerne Courtney. Early versions of the name in the 1500s can be seen in Pimperne and Glanvilles Wootton parish registers. The original meaning is unknown, but is believed to be of French origin.

Farwell - While some people with this name originated from Farewell in Staffordshire, the name is believed to have multiple origins. Other people with the name are believed to have adopted the name for topographical reasons with it meaning 'pleasant stream' in Old English. This spelling is found overwhelmingly in Dorset, with 148 people in the 1881 census residing in the county compared with twenty-eight in Hampshire. In this census, the name is most commonly found in Chideock and Melcombe Regis.

Fooks - Parish registers of the sixteenth century show this spelling variant was only found in Sherborne and Charminster within the county. By 1881 the name was slightly more widespread in Dorset, appearing in eight parishes including Whitchurch Canonicorum, Bridport and Tyneham. The name is Norse in origin from the name *Fulco* and has developed several varieties of spelling and pronunciation since its introduction, such as Folk, Foakes and Volke.

73. *An extract showing the Fooks family of Tyneham from the 1881 census.*

Frampton – This surname has various origins across a few regions in England; those from Dorset are thought to have derived the name from the River Frome with *tun* meaning a settlement. Most commonly found in Hampshire and Dorset, in 1881 the name in Dorset was seen most commonly in Wareham, Gussage All Saints and Portland.

Galpin - In 1881 there were 209 Galpins in Dorset, compared with eighty-three in London and seventy-three in Somerset. At this time the name was most commonly found in Marnhull and Wimborne Minster, but the earliest parish register entry is from Glanvilles Wootton in 1568. The name derives from the Old French word *galopin* and is an occupational name for a messenger or scullion.

Guppy - This is a habitational surname from the hamlet of the same name near Wootton Fitzpaine. Parish registers from the 1500s record the name in multiple parishes including Powerstock, Whitchurch Canonicorum and Maiden Newton. By 1881, the name was most commonly seen in Bridport.

Hansford – This is generally agreed to be a habitational surname, although from which actual place the name derives, no one is quite sure. The most likely options are Hanford in Dorset or Ansford in Somerset. The earliest parish register entry for the name in Dorset is in Sherborne in 1564. Other sixteenth-century entries are found at Abbotsbury and Winterborne Kingston.

Kerley - The origins of this name are much debated and remain unclear. Some believe the name to be of German or Irish origin with others stating the name is a variant of the Kirkland surname. Whatever its true roots, the Kerleys were predominantly found in Dorset and Hampshire in 1881; they accounted for fifty-six per cent of people with the name in England. The earliest parish register entries are found in Milborne St Andrew and Horton in 1580 and 1583 respectively.

Legg – This surname is derived from a nickname given to people who had a distinctive leg or gait. Over 1000 people had this name in Dorset in 1881, most commonly seen in Powerstock. Early findings of the name in Dorset parish registers include 1585 in Allington and 1580 in Wambrook (now part of Somerset).

Loveless – This is a nickname which means *without love*, and some people believe it was originally given to unmarried men. Whilst most commonly seen in Dorset in 1881, the parish containing most Loveless was Portsea in Hampshire, with those in Dorset more spread out throughout various parishes such as Leigh, Tolpuddle and Upwey. The earliest entry in a Dorset parish register is in Piddlehinton in 1583.

Meech - This name is derived from the Old English word *mecca*, meaning friend. The name is spread throughout the county. The earliest parish registers containing the Meech name are in Winterborne Steepleton in 1559. By 1881 the surname was most commonly seen in Bothenhampton, Melcombe Regis and Broadwindsor.

Northover – This is a habitational name from Northover parish in Somerset. In the 1881 census there were 336 Northovers in Dorset, compared with just seventy-four in Hampshire. In Dorset, they were most commonly seen in Swyre, Litton Cheney and Puncknowle. The name was more common in Dorset in the 1500s than most others in this list, with the earliest appearance being 1560 in Symondsbury.

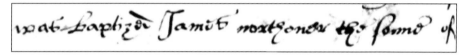

74. *James Northover was baptised on the 19 Dec 1560 in Symondsbury*

Puckett - The true meaning of this name will regrettably most likely never be known. Thoughts as to its origin include a variation of the name Pocket, a form of the Middle English word *pouke* meaning evil spirit or an occupational term for those who made purses. The name is found predominantly in Dorset and by 1881 over a third of those with the name in the county were found in Preston. The earliest surviving parish register examples are from Portesham in the 1570s.

Rideout – This derives from a nickname for horse riders, literally for those who 'ride out'. This spelling of the name is principally found in Dorset. In the 1881 census, 193 people with the name were residing in Dorset compared with just thirty-seven in Somerset and only twenty-five in Hampshire. The sixteenth-century parish registers place the name at Buckland Newton in 1579, with appearances later in the century in Sherborne and Gillingham.

Riggs - A topographical surname applied to someone who lived by a ridge. The earliest Dorset parish register entry for the Riggs name is at Bloxworth in 1586, followed by Winterborne Kingston and Morden in the 1610s. By 1881, the name was most commonly seen in Dorset in Cheselbourne, Puddletown and Fordington.

Stickland – This habitational name heralds from Winterborne Stickland. Stickland itself translates from Middle English into *steep land*. The earliest appearance is in a Dorset parish register at Puddletown in 1545. Other recordings in the 1500s include Dorchester, Rampisham and Winfrith Newburgh. There were 527 Sticklands in Dorset in 1881, with thirty-six in Swanage, twenty-seven in Church Knowle and twenty-six in Cranborne.

Squibb - This is thought to be a name given to those who were witty or sarcastic in their character, although the earliest written reference to the word refers to a firework, throwing doubt on its origin. The earliest parish registers from the county list Squibbs in the 1500s at Cattistock, Gussage All Saints and Stinsford. By 1881, the name was more widespread and covered both Dorset and Hampshire. At this time a majority of Squibbs in Dorset lived in Wimborne, Hilton and Swanage.

Symes – This is a patronymic name for a person whose father is named Simon. The name has now become rather popular across south-west England. It is first seen with the spelling in Dorset parish registers in 1565 in Symondsbury followed by Powerstock in 1568. By 1881, Symes was most commonly found in Bridport and Melcombe Regis.

Turberville - Being a habitational name from Thouberville in France and with no Turbervilles appearing in Dorset in 1881, you may wonder why the name appears on this list at all. Predominantly found in Bere Regis from the thirteenth century, the name had disappeared from the parish by 1780. The Turbervilles resided in Bere Regis manor house during this time, and there is a plaque dated 1559 for Robert Turberville in the parish church. Other Turbervilles can be found in the parish registers for the 1600s in Winfrith Newburgh, Swanage and Puddletown. The name influenced Thomas Hardy's book *Tess of the D'Urberville's*. The name remains very rare today.

Vacher – This is an occupational surname for someone who worked with cows. It is a surname overwhelmingly found in Dorset, and interestingly in 1881, sixty-four of the total of seventy-seven people with the name in the county, were living in Milton Abbas. The remainders were residing in Blandford Forum, Winterborne Whitechurch and Hilton. Early recordings in parish registers are found in Netherbury and Winterborne Whitechurch, with the name featuring very heavily in Milton Abbas from the start of their registers in 1650.

Walbridge - The origin of this name has also been lost over time. It is believed by many to be habitational and to have come from Wool Bridge in East Stoke. Others believe it is simply topographical, referring to a person who lived *near a wall and a bridge*. The earliest parish registers in the county mention the name in Powerstock in 1573 and Askerswell in 1577. By 1881, the name was most commonly seen in Powerstock, Toller Porcorum and Netherbury.

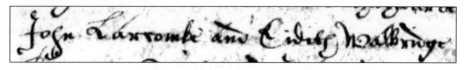

75. *John Larcombe married Eidith Walbridge in Powerstock on 20 Jul 1573.*

Whellar - Thought to be an occupational name for a wheelwright, this surname is one of the rarest on the list, with only twelve people surviving with the name in England in 1881. Eleven of these were in Dorset, residing in Litton Cheney and Symondsbury. The earliest examples found in Dorset parish registers are in Okeford Fitzpaine in 1621 and Trent in 1627.

CHAPTER 23

Dorset Occupations

To a certain extent, many occupations were common throughout England; in almost every county you will find agricultural labourers, servants, soldiers and blacksmiths. However, each county has certain occupations particularly associated with the culture, geography and notable history of the place. For Dorset, many of these occupations are linked to the county's location on the coast, with work involving shipbuilding, rope-making and fishing. Other occupations in parts of the county had strong links to the history of the place itself – such as quarrying in Portland and brewing in part of Dorchester and Blandford Forum – and since Dorset is such a strong agricultural county, you will almost certainly discover farmers and associated trades within your ancestry.

Understanding more about your ancestors' occupations can help you to understand more about their daily lives. For example, researching the farming practices used when your fifth great-grandfather was working as an agricultural labourer will tell you exactly what he was doing. People did not always do the same jobs; occupational practices changed during a lifetime so people had to adjust to an ever-changing world. If an ancestor's occupation changed, it may be of interest to try to discover why. For example, did a whitesmith change their role when they were surplus to requirements? Or perhaps an ancestor left an old job in order to take up an opportunity on the new railways?

Don't forget to research any occupations for your female ancestors too. It is more common for unmarried women and widows to be working than married women with children, although many families found it necessary for both parents to work; in some large families, the older children also worked.

Some common Dorset occupations are listed below. For those not mentioned here, do some research on what they were. There are online resources and books on specific occupations.

Agricultural Labourer

I have yet to come across a family tree based in Dorset which does *not* have agricultural labourers present. Many would rather see professional occupations, such as lawyers or surgeons in their tree, as there seems to be more documentation available for these roles. As soon as people discover that their ancestor was an agricultural labourer, they often cease to research this any further; it is assumed that this commonplace job left no records behind, when instead it simply means we have to use different avenues to understand their working life.

ment.

HEDGING COMPETITION. — A hedging competition, under the auspices of the South Dorset Committee for manual instruction in agricultural processes, took place on Thursday at Came Farm (Mr. J. Passmore's). There were two classes, Class I. for competitors over 25 years of age, who wished to qualify as teachers of the subject, and Class II. for pupils who had received not less than 10 hours instruction. In the first class there were nine entries and in the second three. The work occupied the men from nine till two. As the result of the judging, which was undertaken by Mr. H. Mayo (Dorchester) and Mr. J. Mead (Whitcombe), the following were the awards :—

Class I.—1, £3, George Isaacs, West Knighton; 2. £2 Walter Hatcher, Bincombe ; 3, £1, George Ironside, Winfrith. Class II —1, £2. George Lee, West Stafford ; 2,

76. My great-great grandfather Walter Hatcher, an ag lab, came second in the first class of the Hedging Competition at Came Farm in 1900.

Depending on the period in question, your farming ancestor may be featured in newspaper articles. Local papers often ran articles about agricultural trade unions, accidents on farms, bad harvests and criminal activity such as the theft of livestock. Other more unique articles may also feature, such as fence-making contests or tractor-driving competitions. You may see them described with a more specific term, such as a ploughman, shepherd or dairyman.

All this knowledge helps in understanding more about Britain's social and political history surrounding farming. If your ancestor used to be an agricultural labourer and then changed jobs later in life, this could have been due to mechanisation which greatly reduced the number of labourers needed to work on the farm. Blandford Agricultural Society, just one example, was formed in 1839 and aimed to unite farmers against the hard times they had faced. There was a great deal of discontent amongst many farm workers surrounding low pay and inconsistent work, which led to the Swing Riots in the 1840s when haystacks, farm equipment and machinery were set alight in protest.

Many 'ag labs' lived in tied cottages and therefore moved home when they changed roles. This was common with many labourers given yearly contracts. My paternal grandfather, Thomas Osmond, was a farm worker and he moved with his wife and children several times throughout his working life, including to East Chaldon, Witchampton and Winterborne Clenston. Each property was of a similar, modest size with a small garden where the family grew vegetables. These plots were all similar; my fourth great-grandmother, Hannah Osment in Sutton Poyntz, who is recorded as an agricultural labourer in the 1841 census lived in one much the same. It is less common to find female ancestors working on the farm but certainly not unusual, particularly with women like Hannah, who was unmarried with children to support.

For more recent ancestors, it is worth viewing the 1940 National Farm Survey returns held at the National Archives and described in the Maps chapter in this book. It may be of interest to view other maps from earlier periods to see how the size of the farm changed over time. Visiting the area today can also be of great interest. I personally love to visit the farmlands where my ancestors worked, to see the fields they worked in and to get a better sense of the size of the farm. Carry out searches for any old photographs or even paintings of the farm where your ancestor worked. These may be held by Dorset History Centre, museums such as Dorset Museum or online. Social media can be a great source for old photographs if you join historical research groups.

77. Edwin Percey, an agricultural labourer of Bradford Peverell.

If you are struggling to find specific records for your ancestor, learn more about what a farmer's daily life involved. Being an agricultural labourer was not easy work; it was a very physical role, especially before mechanisation, and labourers had to work long days from sunrise to sunset. After finishing work in the summer there, was little time to do anything other than go home, eat, wash and sleep and get ready for the next day! Accidents were common on farms, but since it was a physical job largely based outdoors, there were health benefits too. By visiting the website of the British Agricultural History Society (www.bahs. org.uk), you can download copies of Rural History Today which contains articles on farming history and provides research tips on a bi-annual basis.

Quarrying

After agriculture, quarrying was the second most important industry in the county, mainly based in Portland and the Purbeck area. Quarrymen may also be known as diggers, quarriers or rock getters and they picked, dug and blasted rock from a designated quarry. Either a crane would then lift the stone to the surface or a cart would be pulled along. Working in a quarry was at best dirty and uncomfortable - at worst dangerous and sometimes fatal. Men would often find themselves having to crouch in one position for hours on end breathing in rock dust, and this was at a time before the long-term health risks of this work were fully understood. Even the most experienced quarrier could have an accident with his work tools, particularly at the end of a long tiring shift. Quarrying was highly physical and exhausting work.

Quarrying on the Isle of Purbeck goes back prior to the Roman period; after the development of improved quarrying methods, an increased amount of stone was quarried in Victorian times. The marble from Purbeck was a popular choice for church fonts and pillars and has been used in Westminster Abbey and Salisbury Cathedral. Portland stone was used to construct countless number of buildings across the country, including key buildings in London such as Buckingham Palace and the Tower of London; the stone was of course used for more local buildings such as the façade of Blandford Town Hall. You can also find Portland stone buildings abroad, such as Leinster House in Dublin, home of the Irish Parliament, and the United Nations headquarters in New York, USA. In the last century, Portland stone was used for war graves and war memorials, including the cenotaph in Whitehall.

There are few surviving records relating to quarry workers, so most of your research into your quarryman ancestors will involve looking at the occupation in generalised terms at the time they were working. HM Prison Portland was opened in 1848 with the initial aim of using convicts to quarry stone. This was a dangerous job and many convicts died whilst quarrying, leading to penal reform. You are more likely to find surviving records of your ancestor if they worked in the quarry as a prisoner, such as via the FindMyPast's collection 'England & Wales, Crime, Prisons & Punishment 1770-1935', which covers Portland inmates.

Fatal accidents—in fact, serious accidents of any kind—are comparatively rare in the Portland quarries, considering the number of men employed and the dangerous nature of the work. Such an accident, however, happened last week to a quarryman named Jonathan Comben Lynham, 46 years of age. He was at work on Monday in one of the quarries in Coombe Field, when a piece of stone, weighing over a hundredweight, fell from a height of 32 feet and struck him on the head. The stone had probably been loosened previously by the crane.

78. The 1899 article surrounding the death of quarryman Jonathan Comben Lynham.

There are many newspaper articles regarding accidents in Dorset quarries. These include the *Weymouth Telegram* on 11 Jul 1899 reporting on the death of forty-six-year-old Jonathan Comben Lynham at Portland quarry and *Blandford Weekly News* on 18 Feb 1892 detailing the death of George Dowland at a quarry in Swanage; both men died after being crushed by falling stone. If your ancestor was working in a quarry at the time of newspaper publishing, try searching for the quarry where they worked in the papers to see if there are any interesting articles from the time. This may give you an insight into the conditions of their daily working life on a particular quarry. The reports are often very detailed about the men's working hours, failures of management and who was to blame for any accidents that occurred.

Brewing

There is a long history of brewing in Dorset going back to 987AD when Benedictine monks were known to brew beer at Cerne Abbas monastery. Brewer's malt came from local barley and you may find ancestors described as maltsters if they helped to make the malt. There were malthouses across the county, including at Weymouth and Marnhull. Beer was then originally brewed at each individual inn. From the early 1800s, breweries started to appear. Male ancestors working here may be described as brewers or brewsters. A female in the occupation may be described as a brewster, brewess or an alewife. A 'broad cooper'- a sort of supervisor - acted as a go-between for the innkeepers and breweries.

Dorchester's largest employer was Eldridge Pope Brewery, established in 1833 and closed in 2003. In 1881, the brewery relocated closer to the railway station, where Brewery Square is today; this move greatly increased the demand for beer and consequently the size of its workforce. The limited company of Eldridge Pope & Co also owned many other sites across the county, such as at Portland, Hamworthy, Sherborne and Wareham. Dorset History Centre holds a large collection relating to the company such as board minutes, trade books, brewing diary books and cash books.

The Hall & Woodhouse Brewery was established by Charles Hall in Ansty in 1777. After Charles' marriage, the brewery amalgamated with Woodhouse's Brewery in Blandford in 1847. They relocated to Blandford Forum in 1900 and they now run tours for the public. This is a great insight into how breweries are run today, as well as learning the history of the industry. Hall & Woodhouse also run a chain of over 250 pubs. Dorset History Centre holds many records related to Hall & Woodhouse including historic photographs and title deeds. Other historic breweries of note are Palmer's Brewery in Bridport, who have brewed ales since 1794 and the Flowers Brewery in Fontmell Magna which dates back to the Victorian period.

Dorset History Centre holds many records relating to other breweries in Dorset

UPON CONDITION, that whereas the above-named *James Cutler Smith of Wimborne Minister aforesaid* is this Day licenced to keep a common Ale-house or Victualling-house, at the Sign of the *Three Lions* in the Parish of *Wimborne Minister* aforesaid, for the Term of One Year only, from the Twenty-ninth Day of *September* Instant.

79. *Excerpt from Ancestry's Alehouse Licence Records showing James Cutler Smith of Wimborne being licenced for the Three Lions pub in 1821.*

including staff newsletters for Devenish Brewery in Weymouth 1968-1985 and title deeds and correspondence for White and Bennett, brewers of Wareham. The Brewery History Society (www.breweryhistory.com) gathers relevant information and photographs and provides a quarterly journal to members that may be of interest to you. Ancestry's collection 'Dorset Alehouse Licence Records 1754-1821' may be of interest to you, particularly in the earlier years when it is more likely that the brewer and publican were one and the same. The licences name the publican and one or two named others, usually men, who acted as sureties for the bond. Not all are indexed so you will need to browse the documents to see if you can find your ancestor. One example dated 14 Sep 1821 names James Cutler Smith of the *Three Lions* pub in Wimborne Minster being granted his licence, with Thomas Barratt of Wimborne as his surety.

Rope and Net-Making
Rope and net-making were common occupations in Dorset, mostly prevalent in Bridport; the source material needed was flax which was grown locally. If your ancestor grew flax, you may find them listed in the 'Dorset Hemp and Flax Growers 1782-1793' list, available on FindMyPast. In the *Universal British Directory* of 1791, there are thirteen companies and men listed as twine merchants in Bridport. In *Kelly's 1895 Directory of Dorset* there were twelve in the same town. If your ancestors came from the Bridport area, you will probably find some working in the industry as it may have been an incentive for them to move there as it was seen as reliable work. Most of the rope and netting made was used at sea, but it wasn't all about maritime industry. A hangman's noose was made of rope - hence the phrase *to be stabbed by a Bridport D*agger came to be used for those who were hanged. Nets were made for sporting uses too including football goals and tennis courts, as well as more intricate goods, such as vegetable bags and the corner nets of a billiard table.

Historically, rope was made on a ropewalk, with workers stretching out yarns to make very long continuous ropes. The yarns were attached to hooks which were then turned by hand to twist them together forming the rope shape we all know

80. *Extract from the Bridport News on 16 Aug 1895*

today. By the eighteenth century, machines were invented to spin the yarns, increasing the amount of rope that could be produced each day. A fascinating article in the *Bridport News* dated 16 Aug 1895 states how highly skilled rope-makers were now little more than *machine minders* and the author worried for the town's future since fewer people were needed for rope manufacture.

Women were heavily involved in the net-making industry with generations of the same family often working together. You may find ancestors in the industry described as net-braiders. Wages were low but it was reliable work that even older children could help with and the work was originally done from home. There are queries today about the impact of the work on net-makers' eyesight, in a similar way that lace-makers suffer. Focusing on intricate work in low-level light would undoubtedly strain the braiders' eyes. There are even reports of blind women creating netting. Eventually machinery was introduced which reduced the amount of labour required. The *Southern Times and Dorset County Herald* on 22 Nov 1884 claims that the first netting machine was introduced to Bridport around 1850.

The British Film Institute has a wonderful film of female net-makers in Bridport at https://player.bfi.org.uk/free/film/watch-rope-and-net-making-in-bridport-1962-online. This shows how quickly the women worked to produce the highest quality netting. Whilst the film is dated from 1962, it certainly gives an idea as to the process that was used and the intricate handiwork that was needed for such a task. Bridport Museum has a collection relating to both the rope and net-making industries, including materials, tools and machinery. They also hold regular demonstrations so you can see how rope was made.

Dorset History Centre has a large collection of records relating to the rope and net-making industry, including the Gundry company of Bridport. Other related sources held here include oral history, photographs and newspaper cuttings. Reports on rope and net-makers feature in newspaper records from the time, although accidents were less frequent in this industry than there were in quarrying.

CHAPTER 24

DNA Testing

DNA testing adds a new science to our research, helping us to prove our family tree is accurate and allowing us to discover new cousins. I have spoken to people over the years who don't believe that taking a DNA test would benefit their research and my advice is always to do one anyway; there really is no harm in trying. There are numerous examples of people uncovering family secrets through DNA results.

The best help it can provide is with regards to adulterous relationships. If a married woman had an affair and became pregnant, she may simply name her present husband as the father on the child's birth certificate or in the parish baptism register and no researcher would ever be any the wiser. Whilst DNA testing works for proving more recent relationships, it will not be able to prove parentage from the 1600s; for that we have to rely on the records alone.

DNA is also obviously helpful in cases of adoption and illegitimacy and can help us learn where we came from. A general rule is to first test the oldest member in your family and then work forwards. If you are the eldest generation in your family, test yourself and your siblings as you will receive slightly different results depending on who has inherited what from your mother's and father's side. The older a person is, the more results they will have but remember, if you are testing a parent, you will only receive matches from one side of your tree.

Ethnicity Results

Finding out about our ethnicity was a huge selling point when DNA testing first became available via genealogy sites – it still is to this day. The truth of the matter is that this science is still fairly new. You will find that by uploading your DNA test to a range of websites, each one will give you different ethnicity results, sometimes varying massively. These sites base their ethnicity research on the samples they have available in their holdings which is why results can vary.

Ancestry has by far the largest DNA database and is therefore often thought to be the most accurate with regards to ethnicity percentages. Websites will update ethnicity results, usually annually, according to their latest research. It is best not to get too bogged down with your ethnicity results because, as crazy as it sounds, this will change as more research is done. Some people are initially told they are ten per cent Scottish, only to have the percentage reduced to zero per cent with the newest update. Base your research on the cousin matches you have, rather than ethnicity results.

81. My father's ethnicity breakdown as of the last Ancestry update on September 2021.

Localised findings are of more use than general ethnicity results. Looking at maps on the ethnicity page will show you dotted community areas. These are results based on your cousin matches and where people in their trees are recorded as residing. Dorset features within the Central Southern England community, which can further be narrowed down currently to 'Dorset and Somerset'. The communities feature can be of more use than ethnicity results as a whole as communities looks largely at the last 50 -300 years, whereas ethnicity goes back much, much further.

Where to Test

Ancestry has the biggest database of DNA results and will therefore be most likely to give you the greatest number of cousin matches. You can also download your DNA from Ancestry to upload to other sites, such as Myheritage and GEDMatch, but you cannot upload a test to Ancestry if you have tested elsewhere. For these reasons, it is usually Ancestry that most people recommend for testing first. Ancestry uses a spit sample to extract your DNA, using a kit that is posted to you.

Other sites that offer DNA testing are Living DNA, My Heritage, Family Tree DNA and 23andMe. As you cannot upload these tests to Ancestry you will not be able to view matches with people who have only tested via Ancestry and not uploaded their results to other sites. Some people still prefer to use other websites for their DNA testing and that is down to personal choice. It may be that you are most comfortable with using My Heritage and are more familiar with their layout. People have had great success through testing with other sites.

Most DNA tests offered by genealogy sites are autosomal, meaning they look at your DNA from both your paternal and maternal sides. If you are only interested in one side of your tree, you may wish to do a Y-DNA or mtDNA test. These are currently available via Family Tree DNA. Only men can complete a Y-DNA test as only they have the Y chromosome that is passed down from man to man through the generations. If you are a woman and wish to know more about your paternal side, test your father or brother. This test only looks at the male line and will not link you to female ancestors.

Both sexes can complete a mtDNA test (otherwise known as mitochondrial test), which looks only at the female line. Rather than looking at everyone on your mother's side, this only looks at your mother, your maternal grandmother, her mother etc. These are great tests to do if you are interested in the specific line. My husband has completed a Y-DNA test in an attempt to discover who his paternal great-grandfather was, as his grandfather Vernon was illegitimate. Whilst there are no results which have helped yet, an increasing number of people are taking them which could provide a new lead any day.

With all DNA tests, I recommend that you don't pay full price. There are frequent discounts available, most notably on Black Friday, Mother's Day and Father's Day, so you can save some money if you can wait. The price has greatly decreased over the years so they are now much more affordable, although be aware there is usually an extra postage fee on top of the price that is advertised.

Interpreting the Results

When you receive your results, make sure you link these to your tree. If you have helped somebody else to complete the test, such as a parent or sibling, ensure you attach these to the right person on your tree. This helps with certain functions completed by the sites, such as Thrulines on Ancestry, where relationships are gathered from other people's trees. It helps to have the most extensive tree possible in order to help with accurate research, and by making your tree publicly viewable, this will help others to confirm their relationship with you and to find a common ancestor. An estimated relationship between you and your matches will be given based on the amount of centimorgans that you share. A parent/child will share around 3500cM and a fourth cousin will share around 35cM. The advice given here relates specifically to Ancestry but the principle is similar for other sites.

Your results will be updated constantly as more people take the test. You will notice that the number of close cousin matches you have will increase gradually as time goes on, with a higher influx usually occurring after Christmas when people who have received them as gifts receive their results. Arrange your results by relationship so you can see the closest relative at the top of the page and work your way down from here. You may already know some of your matches. On my page I am linked to my parents, my maternal uncle and some more distant cousins. You can 'link' these to your tree.

You can choose to filter your results according to those where you have a confirmed common ancestor. For these results, ensure you look at your *matches tree* and the number of centimorgans you share to see if this adds up and makes sense to you. When you know how you are related to someone, you can choose to add them to a colour-coded group. These are private to you and the person who you are putting into a group will not be aware you have done so; it is purely to aid your research. It is up to you how you choose to categorise your results. Most people choose to do this in four groups, one colour for each grandparent, so by looking at your matches list, you can quickly and easily see the line by which you relate to the person.

Once you have tested, you will appear on other people's match lists. But you can choose to keep your test totally private. By making your test and tree public, you may discover cousins who have access to records that help your research and they may provide you with photographs of your ancestors and stories that you would otherwise not have known. Whether to make your results public or private is down to personal choice and how you feel this may benefit or hinder your research.

Where your matches do not have a tree attached to their results, this can make the research more difficult. In these cases, it is worth sending a brief message politely asking if they have a tree you are able to view so you can work out your relationship. You may be able to roughly guess a relationship according to your shared matches, if you are aware of the common ancestor that connects you. Many people receive DNA kits as gifts or purchased them purely to see their ethnicity results. Please, always respect that not everybody will want to find out how you are connected or desire to help you with your tree.

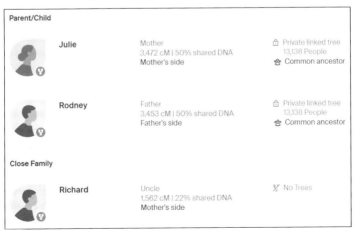

82. My top DNA results showing my parents and my uncle.

It is normal to feel overwhelmed when you receive your results and to rush through each match one by one trying to find answers. People who say that their DNA test hasn't helped their research often do not understand how to best use their results to make progress with their tree. Sometimes by expanding your tree sideways and researching siblings of our ancestors, this can lead to finding cousins and that helps us to go back over time to find common direct ancestors.

If you are disappointed by having few close matches, try not to be disheartened - more and more results are being uploaded every day. In the meantime, whilst you are waiting for a close match, consider encouraging others around you to test. There are examples where people have encouraged their neighbours to do a test, only to discover they are actually related to each other. Go through your matches calmly and methodically and remember that you can always go back to them at a later date.

So, what advice would I give with regards to DNA testing? Buy a test now! Waiting for the results is so exciting and the results can reveal so much information. Make sure you take time to look through your results to understand them. If you're still unsure how to interpret them, ask for help using online forums, social media groups or by hiring a professional researcher. There are also many books about DNA testing and genealogy. And do remember to test older generations first as they will have more of your ancestors' DNA than you do; your parents have about around double and your grandparents around triple.

Dorset Examples

My third great-grandfather Thomas Osment was born illegitimately to Hannah Osment in Sutton Poyntz. A bastardy order held at Dorset History Centre and available at Ancestry names John Puckett of the same parish as Thomas' reputed father. The reliability of these records is questionable as we are often taking the word of the mother, plus that of parish officials who were keen to name a father to avoid paying for the child from public funds. In this case, as the relationship is close enough to provide useful DNA links, my father's DNA results on Ancestry prove undisputedly that John Puckett is indeed Thomas' father. There are multiple links between my father and other people who can link their ancestry back to John or his parents. John's mother has the fantastic maternal name of Squibb which is a delight to trace through both records and DNA due to its rarity.

The story of my great-grandfather Ernest Taylor and his three simultaneous wives is described in the divorce section of chapter sixteen in this book. As Ernest Taylor is such a common name and because he moved between several counties in the south of England, it wasn't easy to prove through records alone that I was researching the correct Ernest.

His third marriage in particular was in doubt. After getting in touch with a descendant of Ernest and his third wife, they agreed to do an Ancestry DNA test.

This proved our theory and showed we are indeed half-second cousins in that we share one common great-grandparent.

Ernest had eleven children with his third wife and none were aware of his previous marriages or the existence of their half-sister, my grandmother Dorothy. DNA testing has thankfully put me in touch with some of Ernest's descendants who have been able to fill in many gaps for me about his life and given me more insight into his character that I otherwise wouldn't have known.

Conclusion

Many beginners in family history start with looking at census records and perhaps the odd birth and marriage record, and then they wonder what to do or where to go next; unfortunately, many just give up and stop researching altogether. This is such a shame because every parish, large or small, throughout the land holds genealogical records of some kind or other. Some parishes have a rich store of ancient records; others have just the minimum. The number of records held by a parish depends greatly on the work and dedication of volunteers who are happy to give their own time to transcribe old documents, registers, wills and many more so that family history research can be made that little bit easier for everyone. Dorset has been lucky over the years – it is one of the counties where interest in family and local history is strong and thriving with many volunteers doing sterling work to help reveal the wealth of information in many records.

Thus, the aim of this book was to produce a comprehensive guide to all Dorset genealogy records for beginners - and even more seasoned researchers - all of whom at one time or another will ask...*but where can I find this? What is in that particular record?*

Remember, genealogical records don't just show names! Together with personal details like names, ages, relationships, places and occupations which can be found on a census, other records contain much more. They reveal details about economic, social and financial information, and provide an important resource explaining the history of the local area too. By providing a fascinating insight of the day-to-day life of everyone who lived in the parish from humble ordinary folk such as farmers, labourers, millers, brewers and rope-makers to more wealthy landowners, clergymen and business people, many records enable researchers to gain a clearer image of who their ancestors actually were by understanding the context of their lives all those years ago. You will often hear seasoned researchers say it is *putting flesh on the bones*!

Beginners can use this book by working through each chapter which hopefully guides you through the process of researching particular documents. More seasoned researchers may perhaps wish to concentrate on chapters regarding more specialised information such as title deeds, courts or manorial records. All records can unlock the secrets of generations of your family ancestry and will help you develop your family tree. This book is designed to approach each record in a systematic logical way, explaining what it is, where you can find it and how valuable it can be to your particular research. I would also urge readers to join the Family History Society of the area that interests you. They can help in so many ways.

People embark upon family history for many reasons - some people have a passion for history, some enjoy the detective side of it uncovering hidden historical secrets and some people just want to learn more about their closest ancestors. Others just want to find the basics – it's all they want to know and it satisfies their curiosity. Basically family history research is all about being resourceful, thinking outside the box and asking the right questions...*why did my mother's ancestors stay in one place all the time yet my father's ancestors are seen in different places doing different jobs?*

Finding the answer to these and many other questions is a bit like doing a jigsaw puzzle; different records reveal lots of information providing all the pieces so that you can complete the jigsaw and see the final picture. Whatever the reason for wanting to find out about your Dorset ancestors, I hope this book will inspire you to discover new records which will enable you to learn more about their lives – and *put flesh on their old bones!* Enjoy your Dorset research!

Image Sources

1. Julie Osmond
2. General Register Office: Weymouth 1924/1/05A/393
3. General Register Office: Weymouth 1861/1/05A/309
4. Dorset History Centre: PE/PRE: RE 1/1-1/2, 2/1-2/3, 3/1-3/7, 4/1
5. The National Archives HO 107/285/15
6. The National Archives RG 11/2103/87/District 4
7. The National Archives RG 9/1348/64/6
8. Dorset History Centre: PE/PRE:RE1/1
9. Dorset History Centre: PE/PRE:RE3/1
10. Dorset History Centre: PE/GIL:RE2/1
11. Dorset History Centre: PE-AFF/RE/4/1
12. Dorset History Centre: PE/OSM:RE1/1
13. Dorset History Centre: PE/BDW:OV5/2/35
14. Dorset History Centre: PE/HIL:OV4/4/1
15. Dorset History Centre: PE/BER:OV5/3/13
16. The National Archives IR 27/156. From FindMyPast; 'Index To Death Duty Registers 1796-1903'
17. Dorset History Centre: AD/DT/I/1757/3
18. Dorset History Centre: AD/DT/W/1795/43
19. The National Archives RG 6/200. From Ancestry 'England & Wales, Quaker Birth, Marriage, and Death Registers, 1578-1837'
20. The National Archives RG 4/303/38. From Ancestry 'England & Wales, Non-Conformist and Non-Parochial Registers, 1567-1936'
21. The National Archives RG 4/1230/13. From Ancestry; 'England & Wales, Non-Conformist and Non-Parochial Registers, 1567-1936'
22. Foster, Joseph *Alumni Oxonienses: The Members of the University of Oxford, 1500-1714*
23. From Author's own family collection
24. Society of Genealogists. From FindMyPast; 'Teachers' Registration Council Registers 1914-1948'
25. *Dorset County Chronicle* 16 November 1865 © The British Library Board. All rights reserved. With thanks to The British Newspaper Archive (www.britishnewspaperarchive.co.uk)
26. Kelly's Directory of Dorsetshire 1880
27. The National Archives IR 1/23 1761 Jul-1763 Dec Page 160.

28. *Sherborne Mercury* 03 January 1846 © The British Library Board. All rights reserved. With thanks to The British Newspaper Archive (www.britishnewspaperarchive.co.uk)

29. The National Archives WO364/1570.

30. Dorset History Centre: L/A/3/5/11/1

31. From Author's own family collection

32. Dorset History Centre: L/A/5/2

33. *Dorset County Chronicle* 29 October 1863 © The British Library Board. All rights reserved. With thanks to The British Newspaper Archive (www.britishnewspaperarchive.co.uk)

34. *Dorset County Chronicle* 16 July 1863 © The British Library Board. All rights reserved. With thanks to The British Newspaper Archive (www.britishnewspaperarchive.co.uk)

35. Reach Licensing/*Western Gazette* 06 Apr 1934

36. Reach Licensing/*Western Gazette* 11 Aug 1939

37, 40. Reproduced under a Creative Commons Attribution-NonCommercial-ShareAlike 4.0 International (CC-BY-NC-SA) licence with the permission of the National Library of Scotland

38. The National Archives IR 29/10/10. From The Genealogist; 'Tithe Apportionments 1836-1929'

39. The National Archives IR 29/10/176. From The Genealogist; 'Tithe Apportionments 1836-1929'

41. Dorset History Centre: QSM 1/24

42. Dorset History Centre: NG-PR/1/D/1/1

43. *Poole and South-Western Herald* 12 March 1874 © The British Library Board. All rights reserved. With thanks to The British Newspaper Archive (www.britishnewspaperarchive.co.uk)

44. Dorset History Centre: NG-PR/1/D/1/1

45. Dorset History Centre: NG-PR/1/D/2/3

46. Author's own

47. The National Archives RG 37/163

48, 49, 50, 51. Author's own

52. Dorset History Centre: Q/D/E(L)/64/45/9

53. Dorset History Centre: Q/D/E(L)/52/14/4

54, 55. Dorset History Centre: D-WIM/JO-1187

56. Dorset History Centre: D1/8306

57. Dorset History Centre: D-WLC/M/86

58. The National Archives Manorial Documents Register https://discovery.nationalarchives.gov.uk/details/c/F244327

59. Dorset History Centre: D-WLC/P/22

60. Dorset History Centre: D-WLC/M/104

61. Dorset History Centre: Q/D/E(R)/3/31/1

62. The National Archives J 77/2104/5884

63. *Poole and South-Western Herald* 23 June 1864 © The British Library Board. All rights reserved. With thanks to The British Newspaper Archive (www.britishnewspaperarchive.co.uk)

64. James O'Shea's family collection

65. Author's family collection

66. Dorset Online Parish Clerks http://www.opcdorset.org/WraxallFiles/Wraxall.htm

67. Rodney Osmond of Bere Regis Village website www.bereregis.org

68. Chloe O'Shea at 'The Past Revealed' www.thepastrevealed.co.uk

69, 70. Author's own

71. James O'Shea's family collection (taken by his grandfather Richard Percey)

72. Dorset History Centre: PE/HAZ:RE1/1

73. The National Archives RG 11/2101/73/District 15/Page 11. From Ancestry '1881 England Census'

74. Dorset History Centre: PE/SYM:RE1/1

75. Dorset History Centre: PE/POW:RE1/1

76. *Southern Times* 24 March 1900 © The British Library Board. All rights reserved. With thanks to The British Newspaper Archive (www.britishnewspaperarchive.co.uk)

77. James O'Shea's family collection

78. *The Weymouth Telegram* 11 July 1899 © The British Library Board. All rights reserved. With thanks to The British Newspaper Archive (www.britishnewspaperarchive.co.uk)

79. Dorset History Centre 'Dorset Alehouse Licence Records' 1821

80. *The Bridport News* 16 August 1895 © The British Library Board. All rights reserved. With thanks to The British Newspaper Archive (www.britishnewspaperarchive.co.uk)

81, 82. Ancestry DNA www.ancestry.co.uk

Images on front cover all author's own or part of James O'Shea's family collection.

Index